PHILOSOPHY

FOR THE BEAST

NICK S DYER

~

Nick S Dyer was at sea for the first seven years of his working life; he trained as a steam engineer on a salvage tug.

After becoming a land lover, he worked as a nightclub bouncer, a prison officer and made several short films for the BBC. Nick has lectured on a variety of subjects at Worcester Cathedral, Oxford University and at Buckingham Palace in the presence of Her Royal Highness the Princess Royal. He is now retired and living in Worcestershire.

Nick's ambitions are to write because people actually enjoy reading his work and live for so many years he becomes a wrinkled, wizened, grumpy old reprobate. Some would say he is well on the way to achieving the latter of these desires.

~

By the same author

TOBY DICKINSON'S NEW DIMENSIONS
The first book of the Daurth chronicles

TOBY DICKINSON'S STRANDS OF TIME
The second book of the Daurth chronicles

TOBY DICKINSON'S TRANSPAR INHERITANCE
The third book of the Daurth chronicles

TOBY DICKINSON'S DARKLIN CONSEQUENCE
The fourth book of the Daurth chronicles

TOBY DICKINSON'S MULTIVERSE OF TIME
The fifth book of the Daurth chronicles

POETRY, MY VERSION
(Out of print)

POETRY MY SECOND VERSION
(Moods for another time)

Non-fiction

FIRST RESORTS FROM A LAST RESORT
A proposition of mandatory systems in the workplace

MANAGING MANAGEMENT
The manager's bible

AN AMERICAN JOURNAL
Ten thousand miles by car and train across the USA

~

PHILOSOPHY

FOR THE BEAST

NICK S DYER

LULU PUBLISHING

Order this book online at www.nicksdyer.com , www.amazon.co.uk and www.lulu.com

Also available from all other major online book retailers for all electronic book systems.

Copyright © Nick S Dyer 2013

ISBN No: 978-1-291-57023-6

Printed in the USA

LULU PUBLISHING USA

■■

Dedications and Thanks

This book is for my children, grandchildren and all the offspring to follow. May the generations be many, healthy and happy.

My sincere thanks to my editor, Peter Dixon. Not only for the fine quality of his work, but still talking to me after examining my conclusions.

~

Contents

~

Foreword

The following chapters attempt to identify a broad definition of where human beings are now and how our development must progress if we wish to have any long-term future.

There is no total analysis of the human psyche, which would take volumes and, I suspect, be so tedious that my reader might lose that wonderful will to live.

Nevertheless, various aspects of the human mind must be mentioned for justification's sake. However, I will try to delve no deeper than Sigmund Freud's lighthearted thoughts over a good breakfast on his day off.

What I see as the major relevant bad points that stop us from reaching a secure potential is more than enough for discussion.

We live on an unstable planet in a complex universe that we understand very little about. If humans are to survive as a species, we must marshal our efforts with much more unity, collective direction and common sense than has thus far been displayed by us.

To support the above premise, throughout the book, I make a number of prescriptive philosophical assertions and statements (PPs* – a précis of which can be found in appendix 1) that support a formula, which offers humankind an assured future.

I dedicate my philosophy to future generations in the fervent hope that they might find some of it useful and exhibit far more wisdom than can be attributed to the human race throughout most of our history.

~

Possibly, one of the most important functions of this book is not only to identify faults, but frailties. There really is a big difference between the two.

For some, my approach may at first seem negative, at the very least. Many may well be seriously offended by the evidence I offer from my view of history and the philosophy I prescribe.

My desire is not to cause offence, or in any way to be sensationalistic. I wish only to provide what I believe is evidential fact while identifying an accurate reality that substantiates my propositions.

One of the hardest skills for any of us to master is the ability to think clearly with only the brain; instead of trying to reach a conclusion while staggering through a thick fog of emotion.

Examine your mind; consider why superstition, fear, prejudice or other feelings might cloud your thinking. Try to only judge the evidence within my words.

Do not misunderstand me. There is a very clear part of life that would be totally incomplete without emotions. Love and all the other wonderful crazy feelings that affect our lives are as much a part of us as existence itself.

However, from a reflective point of view, perhaps try considering how many important decisions you make that are not contaminated by emotion, bigotry or trepidation and are based entirely on common-sense evidence alone.

~

Many of our imperfections, negative habits and practices, have the same constituents as serious addictions.

Our faults and frailties are often deeply ingrained to the point of instinct, or even desirability. To identify those imperfections to someone can be perceived as invasive and highly offensive.

- Nobody can be cured of an addiction without first recognising and accepting that one exists.

This book suggests paradigm solutions for every negative issue identified. However, I openly confess, it will take far more motivated and audacious minds than mine, over a confrontational, protracted epoch, to implement those recommended solutions; although I consider them to be obvious.

I am reminded of Karl Marx. Unlike many philosophers (who Marx considered interpreted the world and existence in various ways then went no further) he believed the point of philosophical conjecture was to change the world. I agree with that conclusion.

Although I feel sure, Marx would have been saddened had he seen the end results of his original concepts. The risk for any innovator is that their ideas will be distorted as the power hungry dictatorial predators swoop.

There are only three absolute certainties within existence. Being born and dying are the first two – and in between? Change. Everything else in life is either a possibility or a probability.

If we fail to control change, it will control us.

'Philosophy for the Beast' sets out a dispassionate mandate for alteration, with the evidence to support reasons for those suggested changes, nothing more.

Make up your own unemotional mind!

All prescriptive philosophical assertions are bullet pointed with the exception of 3 in chapter 1, which are numbered and considered by me to apply to everything within existence.

1

Frailty and virtue

We are the beast; the most predatory killing machine that dwells upon the planet Earth.

We destroy our own kind in a way that no other animal aspires to equal. Constantly, we often drown our judicious intelligence in a sea of destructive, unreasoning, emotion.

Our ability to control feelings is continually subjected to pressures that normal human coping skills are rarely able to manage. So often, sound reasoning is swamped by, among other things: pride, obstinacy, self-importance, a snobbish over-confidence in educational qualification, ignorance, an inability to see an evidential argument above a prejudicial or emotive one and, most damaging of all, insecurity.

- Human kind's greatest fault, frailty and obstacle against evolutional and social development is insecurity.

Despite the occasional acts of selflessness, the motivations of humans are nearly always ruled by self-interest, or putting it politely, something called visual pay value – the, 'what's in it for me syndrome', as psychologists so eloquently describe one of our less attractive, but very understandable natural instincts.

Western and most other modernised society's collective decision making is nearly always governed by financial consideration and the short-term interests of the market economy. Those 'developed' country's leaders suffer from judgments (which are already contaminated by their own ambitions, prejudices and job insecurities) tainted and influenced by faceless money men and women.

Is it any wonder world leaders lack vision and long-term ambitions for the good of all mankind?

Yet human insecurities are far more ingrained, subliminal and influential than those manufactured by the trappings of power and tenuous position.

Have you ever met anyone who was not at sometime influenced in some way by the fear of things unknown?

You know, what we allegedly can't explain, perhaps religion or faith – something greater than us, an all seeing deity – or even things that go bump in the night? If you answer yes to my question, I would find it hard to believe you!

Have you ever met anyone really nice?

Think about it. I do not simply mean someone you particularly like, I mean nice people – a nice person that nearly everyone likes. Sorry to shatter your illusions, such people really do not exist.

Truly nice people are often deceivers who cannot be trusted or weak people who can never really be depended upon. It is because they are nice. They tell you what they think you want to hear, hardly ever having a strong opinion of their own. They smile when inside, quite often, they would rather glare but have not quite got the conviction or courage.

Only rarely will anyone have any idea what nice people are really thinking.

The other side of the coin is the outwardly confident person who couldn't care less whether people like them or not. Their self-belief often extends to a point of brashness coupled with an assertiveness bordering on aggression. Not nice, but usually, if they say they are resolved to do something, they will do it. Leaders perhaps; sometimes charismatic and frequently respected, but never described as nice and rarely liked by a majority.

Those two stereotypical personality extremes loosely describe contentious, but completely opposite characters. They perhaps form a part of a human spectrum that is filled with diverse dispositions; several repeated many times, others that are entirely unique.

No matter how many personalities are catalogued, some will always be missed.

The most important part of any equation, when making a declaration about human beings and the billion facets that make them what they are, and what they may become, is – there are always exceptions.

I say this unreservedly, no matter how many all-encompassing declarations are made by me in my philosophical conjectures, or anyone else has ever made throughout history, upon any subject; there will always be exceptions.

And this leads to the first of my three prescriptive philosophical assertions (PPs) that apply to everything.

1. When contemplating any aspect of existence, the known universe, or infinity; there will always be an exception to any fact discovered, no matter how simple the fact, or how overwhelming the evidence may be supporting the fact. Nothing is ever accurately covered by one sweeping statement. No fact can ever be accepted without the reservation that all things are subject to incremental change, which by definition creates exception.

Yet there are occasions when it is necessary to use all encompassing declarations.

'Everyone dies,' a sweeping statement few would argue with. Perhaps though, it would be more accurate to say, 'as far as we know, everyone dies.' This leads to my second and third all encompassing PPs.

2. There is no totally conclusive evidence existing which suggests that anything is as it has always been, or always will be. No fact is ever entirely unambiguous. A truth today is often tomorrow's lie because acceptable evidence is a continually developing dynamic.

3. All facts depend upon the existence of a reality, which is an entirely subjective and altering entity. Reality, for human beings, cannot exist if someone is not there to observe it. Apparently, everyone's mind

and awareness is different; therefore, reality is only ever a personal singularity.

It is important to establish assertions 1, 2 & 3 and retain them in your mind when considering anything. They are the parameters that must unfailingly be remembered regarding issues that exist now or historically.

- No ostensibly important fact can ever be believed by an intelligent person without viable evidence to support the fact. That burden of proof must be constantly re-examined in a methodical way that includes sound and dedicated practice to readjust pertinent fact so that it matches and supports the up-to-date reality.

For example: Over many years it was an accepted truth by nearly all learned medical men that the practice of 'bleeding' patients (opening a vein and spilling sometimes as much as two pints of blood) improved the 'humours', let diseases flow from the body and was completely beneficial to a sick individual's health. That fact formed part of an important historic reality. Modern evidence suggests that past belief was a load of harmful rubbish.

- Any belief without evidence is an act of pure faith.

My dog was faithful; she was also extremely stupid. There is often little or no evidence at all for some of humankind's most ingrained beliefs. Does that mean that basically, most humans are stupid? Or perhaps, are they simply brainwashed and very insecure?

- I assert that anyone who accepts any serious fact to be true without evidence is perhaps, a fool and if asked, most people would say they would never do such a thing.

- Anyone who does not constantly re-examine any evidence that substantiates something of continuing vital importance – so big that it constantly affects our lives – is perhaps, an even bigger fool.

Acceptable evidence can be as insubstantial as an act of trust.

However, given the duplicity that people are regularly capable of practicing, or the constant mistakes and misinterpretations, both trust and given affirmation must be considered very tenuous at anytime – although, there will always be exceptions.

~

Human beings share many common faults and virtues. Generally, there is an equitable balance within the population that allows a desire and correlation for mutual continued existence.

This collective aspiration for continuation is found in all living things and is, of course, a natural instinct which is surpassed only by the involuntary impulse of perpetuation.

- Ask yourself a question. Why do all living things have an urge to perpetuate the species? It is my belief that there is no one definitive answer, other than natural instinct. We ignore such innate senses at our peril.

- Even life apparently incapable of reasoned thought has the natural instinct to propagate its species. The smaller the intelligence, the more singular are the instincts to survive and multiply.

- Leaving aside the additional in-depth and hypothetical question about an ability to reason, ask yourself, is our planet Earth alive? I believe that it is.

The more intelligent the entity, then the less they are influenced by natural instinct.

In the animal kingdom, a desire to mate is often naturally forced upon the female of the species by dominant males; unpalatable by civilised human standards, but among less intelligent animals, completely natural. Within humans, such instinctive desire is rightly controlled and suppressed.

Our natural instincts are subject to the artificial influence brought about by the rule of law.

Fight or Flight is another natural instinct that humans consistently suppress. The fight rarely develops beyond negative verbal communication and flight usually confines itself to walking away.

Nonetheless, preservation and promulgation instincts can cloud sound reasoning. Even so, the artificial influences of a lawful society usually hold sway.

Emotional Contagion is one more important human instinct that needs to be mentioned. Its original innate purpose probably had something to do with the bonding and self-preservation – tribe forming – necessities of our primitive beginnings.

Emotional Contagion is a tendency for humans to feel and engage with the emotions of people around them. Nowadays it is viewed as a major component of the 'mob psychology' and the 'bandwagon syndrome' (ie:- jumping on the 'bandwagon' of popular conclusion and not thinking things out for yourself).

Emotional Contagion is an instinct that can easily be utilised against the masses when brainwashing techniques are employed (ie: Nazi Germany and the Hitler Youth).

Natural human instincts are a part of our being. But many of them have been bastardised and mutated beyond their original purpose. The foundation of those alterations is undoubtedly our sophisticated development and artificial, technological environment.

Nevertheless, our instincts still retain some important functions; but they also exercise tremendous influence in many negative ways.

The further intellectually proficient and technologically sophisticated we become, the less our true natural instincts influence our lives. But possibly the mutated instincts contribute towards a growing unequal balance of emotions and insecurities that, as yet, we are not fully aware of and therefore are incapable of managing successfully.

Natural human instincts and emotions are valuable assets we should never neglect. They are a part of whom and what we are. However, as with all unreasoning, unconscious instincts and emotions, we must continually be aware they exist and frequently hold sway upon us.

The manipulation by the unscrupulous of unconscious human response is something that must never be forgotten.

So many modern customs and practices of humanity are dictated by unreasoned and illogical instinctivness rather than evidential considerations.

Science is not to blame.

Without science human civilisation is doomed. Whether we like it or not, science is responsible for virtually everything in our day-to-day lives.

Emotional Contagion has nearly always been used by the dictator, the fanatical and the anarchistic. Might it not be time that such an obviously influential natural instinct was used for the positive manipulation of all humanity?

~

The balance of fault and virtue in world society is supported artificially by the rule of law.

Whether the laws of all countries and cultures are just will always be a matter for conjecture and amendment. But the strived for ideal is that those laws can only be enforced with the substantiation of evidence and the acceptance of a majority.

I suggest that laws are very worthwhile standards, and the only logical conclusion for all societies that any intelligent person can accept.

- The rule of law is probably the greatest virtue the human race possesses.

Diving on barrier reefs and watching coral fish is a comprehensive way to observe a miniature representation of every other living creature on our planet and how they interact without the rule of law.

Most reef fish are easy prey for predators if left in an exposed situation.

The living coral provides protection. While some fish act as soldier-lookouts, others provide food or cleaning services for the coral.

All the reef fish contribute in their way, but it is a hazardous existence at best and predators attack at will.

There are clear comparisons with a barrier reef and what was once known as the Wild West in the United States of America. Organisation of a kind, but until the rule of law was enforced systematically in the frontier territories, guns and working together for mutual survival was the dominant procedure.

Only the predator stood alone in such situations, and of course, largely did as they liked.

As a consequence of the predator, all creatures seek security and support from others of their kind. It takes very little historical alteration for a predator to become a dictator.

- Fish shoal, other animals herd for protection, and where the rule of law does not exist in a comprehensive and totally accepted way, humans tribe.

Without the law, it is very much, survival of the fittest.

Law has given nations a reasonably stable society and harmonious existence in many areas of the world.

The rule of law has probably been the most civilising influence on human beings that has ever existed.

However, the system is far from perfect and the balance of justice that the law is meant to provide is often tremendously subjective. Frequently the legal system is misused and over-complicated by those who purport to represent it.

- The law must be nurtured, protected, unambiguous and never taken for granted; the more complexity the greater the insecurity.

The rule of law has existed in varying forms for thousands of years. Whatever their form, laws have greatly contributed to our synthetic way of life.

'Survival of the fittest' and 'law of the jungle' are cruel and unreasonable but apparently, completely natural.

The rule of law is artificial but strives to be fair and a virtue. Perhaps it is the first step upon the long, intricate road of self-determination and advancement for mankind.

~

An increase in human insecurity can be clearly observed in every aspect of our daily lives.

Early twentieth century children played outside nearly all day if not attending school.

Old people would happily leave their homes and regularly go out for the evening, perhaps to a public house or cinema.

Both age groups walked the streets, in the main, without fear. By the late twentieth century those practices were very rare.

Have the dangers to those sections of society increased?

I would suggest they have, but only relatively. The larger the population, so the percentage of perpetrator and victim rises. What has increased beyond any of the other figures is insecurity.

- Insecurity is humankind's greatest frailty.

- The governing authorities and people of power and influence in all the countries throughout the world, either intentionally or unintentionally, aggressively or subliminally, constantly feed humanities' insecurities.

Fear is an extreme insecurity, but also, a completely natural instinct.

A good example of mutated instincts is perhaps the proposition that the only fear that exists today, unchanged from the time that the first humans set foot upon the Earth, is the fear of death before reproduction has taken place.

However, the modern mutations of the fear of death are numerous.

Sophistication has led to many new fears where demise is concerned. Among other things, we now understand what many illnesses are, complete with their terminal conclusions, and how we might suffer for a protracted period.

Ignorance truly was bliss.

- The more we know about everything, the greater the fears and insecurities that accompany that awareness.

- The more we depend upon the unsubstantiated words of leaders and other influential individuals to feed our ingrained superstitions, the more insecure we become.

- The greater the insecurity, the bigger the emotional response.

Not only does knowledge increase insecurity, complexity of life and artificialdom breed anxiety as well. Quite often, the very laws and regulations designed to protect us feed our doubts and fears.

Health and safety is worthwhile legislation calculated to protect and cause dangerous practice to cease. But it appears to have created a frightened 'nanny state' within

Great Britain. In many schools, children have been banned from playing on swings or climbing frames.

The age old tradition in English schools of playing conkers has suffered an almost countrywide ban. Many older people express feelings of having bred a generation of 'wimps'.

Certainly, according to figures supplied by the Department of Health, young people suffering from neurosis and other mental health problems has increased markedly over the last four decades.

- The workplace suffers from increased insecurity. Market forces, meeting targets and continually increasing profits have become Gods.

- Percentage wise, there are more people consulting psychiatrists and psychologists in the western world than there have ever been.

- Insecurity has caused abortive tribalistic, cultural and religious reliance that breeds divisiveness.

- Without otherwise altering feelings or emotions, were it possible to take away tribalism, cultural differences and religions, there would be no racism, only likes and dislikes.

- The divisiveness of culture, race and religion are some of the greatest manufacturers of insecurity.

~

Quantum mechanics describe the ability to be in two places at once. So it is for mankind.

We stand on the threshold of a golden age; our technology really is capable of far more than we collectively ask of it. But at the same time, we are looking into the entrance of an abyss that will see the end of the human species as we know it.

No matter how painful it might be at first, we have to embrace the concept that humanity must change.

One of the major facts humankind must face is that, left almost entirely in an artificial world society depending on the whim of entrepreneurial leadership, consumer generated profit and separatist development, the human race is probably doomed within the time set of only a few generations. The evidence to support such a statement is overwhelming.

Throughout history, empires, individual countries, national economies and multi-national organisations continually transform from success to failure – ad-infinitum. Each time the cost of such practice can be measured by tremendous waste and social upheaval. More often than not, those alterations are the responsibility of just a handful of people, or even only one person.

While many leaders and entrepreneurs may be idealists with selfless principles and visions, many have only greed, vanity and a hunger for power as their motivations.

However, no matter what the reasons, everyone that influences change from an entrepreneurial situation does so from a position of personal ambition, skills, prejudices and insecurities that usually disregard considered long-term responsibilities.

Quite often, organisational or national success suffers with the end of an individual's professional or actual life.

Entrepreneurialism has always been attractive to the ambitious, lovers of freedom and self-determination. But it is fraught with the faults, whims and frailties of the imperfect human individual.

Entrepreneurs are innovators the world could never be without, but like America's Wild West needed law and order for long term civilisation, innovators need system.

- Where entrepreneurialism has influence or a significant effect over a large majority, such effect must be underpinned by a firm foundation of systematic practice that becomes more regulatory and influential than the originating entrepreneur.

Although mostly barbaric and unacceptable by today's standards, the Roman Empire endured successfully for hundreds of years because it had been systemised.

Roman systematic customs and practices became recognisable to millions spread over three continents.

Some of the Roman systems still exist today. Indeed, the only time that mighty empire experienced setbacks during its history was when an individual gained too much power.

- Global systemisation is the most logical and positive progression the human race could embrace.

Only the security of system allows the virtues of people to be successfully developed and the frailties of humankind to be supported to a point where those individual shortcomings no longer have significant influence.

Benefits of systemisation will be discussed further in later chapters, but before contemplating any kind of solution to humanity's problems, the full extent of dilemmas besetting our future must be identified and examined.

2

God

Perhaps it is a very sad indictment that the frailties of mankind need a metaphoric shoulder to cry on – someone or something greater than ourselves that we can call upon when there is no other alternative; a parental figure that can wave a magic wand and make everything right when our feeble minds cannot cope.

What a collectively inadequate, neurotic and pathetic sample of life we are.

If humans truly are the superior race on Earth, then conceivably, the miracle of life is not the wonder it first appears.

Surely it is time we learned to walk without the aid of a spiritual crutch.

Doubtless we should be grateful for our existence and always acknowledge the vast amounts we do not know, but not forever contemptible dependants. Nobody owes us anything.

Nor should we be subservient.

If humanity truly does hold a belief in God, then they really need to properly consider that conviction and look for the common-sense within it, not the mystic superstition of our forefathers.

Remember how in ages past people worshiped the sun and thought it some kind of deity? Today we would label such belief as naïve at best and realistically, based on superstitious ignorance.

Remember, we are not equal as human beings; to say otherwise is simply political correctness and utterly ridiculous. It does not matter.

- Every human is as good as each other and are born with a right to be here.

To worship anything or anyone with a faith bordering on the blind reliance of a household pet is utterly demeaning and against all of humanity's instincts.

Yet the concept of God exerts tremendous influence upon humankind.

Prior to discussing the more controversial subjects of religion and culture, it is perhaps wise to look at the evidence for or against the existence of God and then maybe, consider exactly what God might be.

Simone Weil (1909 – 1943) a French philosopher, struggled for a long time about her belief in God. She was nicknamed the 'Red Virgin' for supporting communism and presumably, abstinence in some areas of her personal life as well.

Best known for her support for the working classes, Simone studied continually, trying to comprehend the real needs of workers while at the same time, attempting to quantify her spiritual convictions.

Although born a Jew, she briefly flirted with Catholicism before considering spiritual mysticism.

T. S. Eliot called her a genius. Whether or not Simone was that clever is perhaps not for me to judge. But she said one thing that I read as a teenager, thought very wise, and it has stayed with me ever since.

"I have looked for God for the greater part of my life and have formed one conviction. God has entirely nothing to do with religion."

With Simone's point about God and religion, I am in complete agreement.

Throughout history, there have been dozens of highly intelligent men and women who have believed in God. Yet many of them experience great difficulty when it comes to explaining why they do.

Some rely almost entirely upon the evidence of the scriptures and other religious books. I find such reliance and acceptance amazingly naïve – to say the least.

"It's astonishing how you can start believing in God when you're really scared."

That statement is an extract from a letter sent home by a soldier in the trenches during world war one.

~

Throughout much of my working life, part of my job was the gathering of evidence. I have witnessed serious incidents that involved complex criminal prosecutions.

The worst case scenario is when there are no witnesses. The second worst case scenario is when there are too many witnesses.

Quite often, it is impossible to obtain agreement about what happened. Sometimes it is even possible to get a witness who, convinced they are telling the truth, swears that nothing at all happened.

Evidence gathering from witnesses can take place minutes after an incident and also as an ongoing process when minds have supposedly cleared of shock, other reactive emotion and after observers have had time to think about what occurred.

Eventually, some kind of evidential picture will emerge and is usually accurate enough to be relied upon. Nevertheless, it is almost impossible, without the aid of close circuit cameras, sound equipment and a professional analyst, to gain a completely accurate picture.

Evidence gathering is a science that has been perfected over the course of many years' hard work by dedicated people who have had a mountain of incidents upon which to hone their craft.

On the other hand, we have 'the scriptures' etcetera. Those documents have been translated and interpreted many times through the ages.

Some were written approximately two thousand years ago, while others are even older. Those writings were recorded by apparently untrained men of unknown intelligence.

In the case of Christianity, allegedly, some of them were fishermen and still others manual craftsmen. These men are usually revered and have, in some branches of

Christianity, been canonised. I have no wish to disrespect them in anyway, but I wouldn't trust the accuracy of their continually reworked statements about anything.

St Thomas Aquinas (1225 – 1274) was a man of religion and a philosopher of highly respected reputation. He attempted to reconcile Aristotelian and Christian thinking while at the same time maintaining a distinction between faith and reason.

However, neither his faith (which was obvious) nor reasoning (which was clever and well constructed) provided any proof for why he believed in God.

About four months before his death, Thomas declared he had some kind of cathartic religious experience. Following that occurrence he then stated:-

"All that I have written seems to me like straw, compared to what has now been revealed to me."

Well, again, it's a shame Aquinas didn't bother to share his experience and reveal it to us.

John Duns Scotus (1266 – 1308) is considered to be one of the greatest metaphysicians (a branch of philosophy which examines and explains the ultimate nature of everything in existence) that ever lived.

He posed the, probably far from original question, 'Does God exist?' His answer was seen as the crowning achievement of his work.

Extremely complex and intellectualised, his metaphysical argument declared that God must exist.

His main body of proof appears to be arguing backwards from the effects that God has on everything (if that's not subjective I don't know what is) so he must exist.

Clearly a very intelligent man, but so far removed from evidential fact and sound common sense, he might just as well not have bothered.

Probably the best argument for God existing, and one that is far more simplistic, comes from an Archbishop of Canterbury.

St Anselm (1033 – 1109) put forward a most uncomplicated theory, with what he saw as evidence. His basic precept was: because the concept of God exists now and has seemingly always existed in some form or another, it is self-evident that God exists as well.

St Anselm's ontological argument sits well with my theory about reality.

If enough people believe something to be true, then until they (or a future population) decided otherwise, that is the factual reality.

Considering his declaration dates back to the beginning of the twelfth century, it certainly has stood the test of time. St Anselm's concept is as relevant today as it has always been since he first wrote the words.

But is St Anselm's argument evidential? Does it offer conclusive proof?

As much as I like his postulation, I think the answer to both questions is no. Nevertheless, were there no better evidential statement to support the existence of God, I would probably be inclined to accept his evidence.

However, I suggest a far better argument exists for the reality of God with a great deal of evidence.

Every now and then, some highly qualified individual hypothesises about how the universe began.

The current most popular theory is the 'big bang' and at the time of writing this tome, scientists have allegedly discovered the, somewhat irreverently named, 'God particle' which, according to those scientists, started 'the bang'.

A significant amount of, apparent, evidence exists to support the 'big bang' theory – mostly mathematical. It is true to say that the majority of mathematic formula, when relating to the universe, apparently proves to be broadly correct.

However, as Sigmund Freud once remarked:-

"It is all very well obtaining the correct answer to a question. But if the question is wrong in the first instance, the answer is wholly irrelevant."

At the risk of being accused of using Freud's comment as a cliché, let me reinforce his words with this evidence: we cannot prove conclusively when life started on Earth, if the planet Mars ever sustained life, or how the asteroid belt between Mars and Jupiter came into being.

All we have is speculation. If science cannot be definite about our own planet and the objects closest to us, how can we possibly accept any sweeping statement regarding the whole universe?

- There are always massive omissions with all the 'how everything started' theories and the accompanying equations.

It is my belief that every intelligent and learned person has a right to seriously speculate on the beginning of existence and then, if their conviction or narcissistic urges compel them, publish those suppositions. But they should be very clear when making declarations what exactly they are; nothing more than intellectual speculations, usually devoid of any understandable fact or physical substantiation, which could reasonably be accepted as evidence.

There are questions that always remain unanswered by academics.

If time, the 'God particle' and the whole universe started with the 'big bang', where did the nothing come from to put it in? And where did the 'particle' come from? And how did the particle expand to form a universe of immeasurable size? And finally, what made it become critical and go bang?

- No sound, complete, evidential argument exists for how the universe began; where the constituents (God particle among other things) came from to start it, or how the space materialised to put it all in.

- I suggest there are two indisputable pieces of evidence that, at this time (2013) undoubtedly prove the reality of God to me.

On a clear dark night, stand outside in an unlit area and look up. You will see the physical evidence of the most incredible miracle anyone will ever see.

The endless stars contained within billions of galaxies that visibly exist in the forever we call infinity.

Our universe is apparently, without conclusion.

We have less of a comprehensive explanation of what it is, how it began or where it ends than an amoeba has about the complexities of relativity.

I believe the universe and everything in it to be the physical representation of God.

Nothing else could possibly account for such obvious omnipotence. It is the most wonderful, magnificent, phenomenon. How it works, if it thinks, what purpose it serves, what part we are meant to play within it are all mysteries that are completely incomprehensible at this stage of human development.

And therein lays the true meaning of creation for me.

Charles Darwin (1809 – 1882) believed: "life is a continually evolving and developing medium."

- In the absence of any other evidential argument or rationalisation, the universe is God and is entirely inexplicable.

- Several philosophers' support the theory that the universe must have been created by God – just like a beautiful painting must have been created by an artist – nothing begets nothing, not something.

The other piece of evidence I offer for God's existence is the miracle of awareness through being.

Many philosophers have hypothesised about awareness (I think, therefore I am) or the possibility of illusion (only the moment exists and that could be part of a computer programme. The future does not exist and never will and the past and present is but an illusion or dream). Even if we only ever have the present, it is enough.

If the universe is the physical manifestation of God, then despite our bodies, existence is the non-physical; it is the spiritual manifestation of God – because we (our bodies) are not existence, but only the witnesses to it.

Life (the electricity – energy – spirit – force) itself is what makes the physical body work and I have yet to find anyone who can explain exactly what life is.

Our bodies are probably a result of random selection. Charles Darwin's theory of evolution supports the proposition that God created life itself, not all the animals and insects one by one. I find myself agreeing with that conclusion and there is considerable evidence to support Darwin.

After all, what kind of a God would it be that deliberately created mosquitoes?

Reality only exists because of us. We only subsist because of existence itself. Like the universe, there is no alternative evidential argument to explain existence other than, God is existence.

These two pieces of evidence lack one coherent fact to give them total credibility. They do not describe entirely what God is. That point is the most beautiful irony of all; because God is entirely inexplicable, God becomes whatever you want him/her/it to be.

God is everything – several philosophers have already made that point in the past. What they did not say was, that being everything, God is whatever you want him (yes, I prefer him) to be.

If you want a wise looking old man with long white hair and beard sitting on a golden throne who likes to be worshiped every Sunday, then that is the way God is.

At the same time, for the slightly masochistic, if you want a God who will burn you in hell's fire for all eternity because you succumbed to the odd moment of coveting, then good luck, he's all yours.

- God is a comfort. He's the old rag you chewed and held close as a child. He's the mystical being up in the sky who gives you a mental cuddle when you're scared witless. He must be contextualised as wholly incomprehensible and therefore only ever a very personal reality.

I am not trivialising God.

There is a very serious point to the above paragraphs. If you believe in the physical miracle of the universe, and the spiritual miracle of existence, and that those two miracles are inexplicable and beyond understanding – rather like the mathematical number *pi*'s final figure – God is everything, and whatever you decide is your reality, then that is God.

- Do not blame God for what you think he is or what you do with your portion of existence. If you can conceive God from the irrefutable substantiation I have illustrated, then you are responsible for your version of him.

I believe there to be no better evidential explanations for God, neither physical nor psychological, or even philosophical substantiation, than I have described.

I suggest any other concepts of God are either inexpressible and beyond any human ability to understand, or ancient tales lacking any common sense or up-to-date credibility.

Arguments about God or the Devil, good and evil, love and hate, or every other facet of existence are irrelevant, save for the accountability of how we use those facets and how we choose to implement them. We know they exist – our responsibility, our preference – with no mystical third party who shares the blame for our actions; other than having allowed creation in the first place.

All sensation and experience are a part of existence, nothing more or less.

- God is not a crutch to lean upon (we have minds of our own, so use them) but perhaps believing is a comfort when no other subsists.

- God is not an excuse to blame when things go wrong – we control enough of our lives and command enough factual evidence to know we humans or our unstable world and solar system are responsible.

- Look no further for an explanation of God, you will not find one.

There is no doubt in my mind at all, my God exists, but he may well not be your God.

However, no matter what our beliefs, they must be contextualised and used as a personal experience only to be shared, perhaps upon request, but never imposed on others as a way of life.

I suggest dogmatic belief about anything that lacks the substantiation of acceptable evidence is perhaps the act of someone who has been brainwashed, is insane, or a complete idiot incapable of coherent thought.

And I pray that my God agrees with me!

3

Religion

The greatest solace for mankind's insecurities throughout history has been religion; it was deemed to be the manifestation of God's laws and a way of living dictated by him.

In many ways, religion was the first bringer of the law and where it was not, faith usually gave its support. Religion was a civilising influence in most areas of the world and brought order out of chaos.

A. Religion gives hope of a better life in the hereafter, where people will meet God and enjoy an eternity of wonderful experiences.

B. It gives comfort, companionship and a sense of belonging to those that need it.

C. Religion gives everybody who 'believes' a sense of direction and reassurance to ease their multitude of fears and insecurities.

D. All the world's major religions support a belief in some version of God.

Those are the good things. However, in today's world, the positive is far outweighed by the negative.

A. Religion has become more influentially divisive and sectarian in the modern world than perhaps it has ever been.

B. Religion is a seemingly accepted excuse and sanctuary for despicable criminal actions.

C. Religion is culturalistic and by its very dissimilar doctrines, a major cause of tribalism.

D. Today's religion has little or nothing to do with God and far more to do with political ambition and culturism.

E. Collectively, religions are institutions of secrecy, and organisations for amassing vast wealth and power.

F. All major modern religion discriminates against women.

G. There are restrictive dress codes plus limited social and educational opportunities compulsorily practiced on females in many parts of the world in the name of religion.

H. Forced or arranged marriages and even physical mutilation are other inhumane acts women are subjected to as a result of restrictive religion-dictated cultures.

I. Religion often provides an excuse for inhumane acts that any decent person should be appalled by.

~

Consider Christianity; collectively by far the biggest of the religions with well over two billion devotees.

Catholic and Protestant are the two biggest factions within the Christian world and when they're not arguing or even at times trying to kill each other, they seemingly unite to discriminate against women.

a. When did you last see a female Pope or Archbishop of Canterbury?

Christianity is a male dominated domain still broadly living in the dark-ages.

Christianity's language is often an aberration of Latin, Old-English, or a badly phrased parody of any indigenous tongue depending on what part of the world is experiencing its rituals. As a result, many of the prayers, incantations, psalms and Bible texts are quite meaningless to modern generations.

All of that abortive verbalisation would not matter very much if it were not for the negative influence it exudes.

Catholicism in particular discriminates against women forbidding them the benefits of contraception or divorce in direct contradiction to the laws in many countries.

They will not allow women to hold high office within the church; in that matter Protestants are little better.

Yet society as a whole accepts these discriminatory acts; although I feel sure, they are in direct contradiction of laws against discrimination.

> **b.** How many cases of sexual assault and other crimes committed by its clergy has the Christian church covered-up or attempted to minimise?

Again the law is flouted by Christianity.

More worryingly perhaps is the fact that none of the so-called enforcers and guardians of our law appears willing to enforce the edicts against the Christian church.

How many secrets does the Vatican hide within its walls that are deemed not to be suitable for the eyes of ordinary mortals? Why can't we see them?

Or are the Vatican secrets no more than tales that hint of a mysticism designed to feed the insecurities of humans?

While mysticism might be one controlling manifestation of Catholicism, the English Protestants can claim that, thanks to Henry the eighth's sexual excesses, their church has far more physical motivations for membership.

But look at its influence, then ask yourself, where is the common sense reasoning and decision making among an, allegedly, democratic populace that such unchecked power and control has been allowed to develop and sustain itself, even to this day?

c. How much wealth does the Christian church erroneously control while millions of its followers starve and suffer throughout the world?

Most Christians believe that Jesus Christ was the son of God and his Mother Mary was a virgin. One should perhaps consider husband Joseph's position, but if I do that I will be accused of being completely sacrilegious.

Nevertheless, I feel bound to point out that there is not a shred of evidential proof that any of this implausible story is true. It is a matter of pure faith. At the risk of repeating myself, my very loveable dog was faithful.

The life of Jesus Christ is well documented. Unfortunately, most of that documentation is recorded from word of mouth stories – much of it after he was dead.

I would predict those stories suffered from the same evidential discrepancies that I described when mentioning the professional gathering of evidence.

His crucifixion is probably the most evidential fact about Jesus. Allegedly, he was sentenced to death for claiming to be the King of the Jews and generally upsetting the tribal Jewish Elders.

The tragic fact is, the Romans would crucify any non-Roman for the sake of expediency or who offended them in the slightest way. There would have been nothing remarkable about a perceived troublemaker being nailed to a cross in those days.

The amount of people crucified by the Romans numbered into thousands, perhaps even millions. Their version of society dictated that they often lined the Apian Way with crosses. Over six thousand were crucified in one disgusting orgy of enforcing Roman will during the year 71 BC.

> **d.** In the Middle East, there are countries still using crucifixion as a means of judicial punishment now, in the 21st century.

Sadly, crucifixion was the barbarism said to have ended the life of Jesus – nothing out of the ordinary in those days. What the real (if any) significance of it was, we will never know. Evidentially, it is the stuff of legends and purely a matter of faith.

My opinion is that if Jesus did exist. He was probably a charismatic man who wanted to make life better by turning a barbaric society towards a more humane path. History is laced with such legendary heroes who try to free an enslaved people or improve their collective lot.

Unhappily, people have a way of recording what they wish had been and not what really was; especially when an enslaved nation is looking for a saviour.

Perhaps the last word on my observations about Christianity should be left to one of its most senior representatives.

Pope Benedict XVI stated, "It sometimes felt as if God is asleep."

All credit to him for such a candid revelation regarding his feelings upon his, most unusual, retirement – forgive my scepticism, but so much for Christian faith!

~

Possibly the biggest irony of all is the fact that most of the witnesses to the life of Jesus Christ were Jews and they (as a majority) do not believe in him. Judaism asserts quite clearly that Jesus was not the son of God.

The Jewish holy book called the Torah, claims uniqueness for the beginning of Jewish faith. It states Judaism is the only religion that does not depend on a personal revelation given to one individual, who, they say, might be delusional or lying.

According to the Jewish religion, their faith began with a revelation when God allegedly spoke to over two thousand people from Mount Sinai.

But that was thousands of years ago, before Jesus, Muhammad or Buddha were ever thought of – and nothing since?

To me, the happenings on Mount Sinai are also the stuff of legends and leave far more questions than answers.

Again, after all this time, one can only declare that just like Christianity, Judaism is nothing more than a matter of faith and a tribalistic way of life, depending on the level of devotion.

~

The second biggest religion in the world is Islam, with about one and a half billion followers.

Islam began in Mecca. A revelation is believed to have been passed from God to the angel Gabriel who gave it to a man called Muhammad.

Muhammad was born in either 570 or 571 AD.

After allegedly marrying into a wealthy family and devoting his time to philosophical pursuits, by the year 621, following the revelation, Muhammad was being persecuted for his beliefs. A group from Medina pledged themselves to him and declared they would defend him with their lives – they called themselves Muslims.

Islam went from strength to strength. By the time Muhammad died in 632, he had established a religion and social order that still flourishes today.

Although Muslims would have the world believe they are a united religion, rather like Christians, they are split into two major factions, Shiites and Sunnites. Like the Catholics and Protestants, they often argue and try to slaughter each other.

Besides various other documentation, the version of the Qur'an I studied was the translation by Abdullah Yusuf Ali (1872 – 1953).

Translations, just as historical rewrites, always result in a loss of originality.

Nevertheless, I find the contents of the Qur'an to be far more uncompromising than most religious books. It dictates an obdurate and sectarian way of life. Hell's fire and brimstone await transgressors, or heaven with all its perceived rewards for those who are mindlessly obedient.

Owing to the way it sometimes contradicts itself, the Qur'an is open to many differing interpretations. Those interpretations have been used to dictate a culture that has given birth to some of the worst intimidation and acts of terrorism the 20th and 21st centuries have seen.

For the sake of succinctness, my notes about Islam are very brief. As you might expect, there is far more to its beginnings and Muhammad's history, but the salient points are covered.

The most important issue is, like Christianity, Islam depends upon the unsubstantiated word of one man. Yet again, there is no evidential proof that we can rely upon. Once more we have a religion that requires faith, because by today's standards, there is nothing else.

Nevertheless, such are the insecurities and discontent of so many individuals throughout the world, Islam is the fastest growing religion today (2013).

The motivations of the current converts are often complex and highly politicised. But whatever they may be, those motivations appear to have very little to do with God or the intrinsically spiritual good that Islam purports to engender.

Sharia law (the law which many Muslims choose to live by) often inflicts a barbarism upon perceived perpetrators that has no place in a modern, intelligent, society.

So ask yourself, why does Islam attract so many modern converts?

Are there so many disenfranchised people that they would support something often so extreme rather than the supposed benefits of democratic Western society?

Or is something far more contrived and surreptitious at work?

I would suggest that there is.

~

There are about twenty-two major religions. I make the figure an approximate one because the powers that be cannot ever agree exactly how many there are.

If the rules of a British Census are applied, then being a Jedi (characters from the George Lucas Sky Wars franchise) with or without a light-sabre, must be recognised.

By the same token, Rastafarianism should also receive credibility. Although I cannot help but wonder if smoking cannabis really does help contact the dead Ethiopian Emperor, Haile Selassie.

From the oldest recognised religion (which apparently is a toss-up between Hinduism and Judaism, give or take a thousand years or so) to, allegedly, the youngest (probably Scientology – good old L Ron Hubbard, I read all his science fiction books as a child, they were far-fetched as well) not one of them offers a shred of evidential proof that would stand up to unemotional and unbiased scrutiny.

It is a frightening thought to face the fact that religion is perhaps nothing more than fanciful legends; fictitious tales that ridiculously hold a sway upon so many intelligent people, simply because their basic insecurities will not allow them to face life without such obdurate support.

> **e.** Most religions, intentionally or unintentionally, feed and prosper from the insecurities of mankind.

~

Let me take you to the drab smoke-filled cities of Germany during the 1930s.

I am constantly sickened by the modern excuse that it was not the Germans that tried to murder every Jew in the world and enslave nearly everyone else.

It was the Nazis!

What utter rubbish, but a fine example of how handed-down history alters itself for the sake of expediency.

Have you ever seen the film footage of a Nazi party rally?

Those old news movies are probably the most accurate take on that period of history. It looked like an awful lot of Germans happily taking part to me. All of them shouting and cheering, clicking the heels of their boots, with one arm sticking out palm down in front of them, as Adolf Hitler and his uniformed goons postured.

Never to be forgotten were the cream of Germany – the youth. And here we find the first clue to how so many preposterous and dangerous dogmas take root, because they were not just the German youth. They were the Hitler Youth – a product of brain-washing, propagandist education through the schools and media of the day.

The youth of Germany were enthused with tales of tribal patriotism, nationalism, racial superiority and a collective joy of belonging to something that made them stronger than their individual insecurities would have ever allowed them to be.

You may not like the comparison between religion and Nazi-Germany, but it is a very clear and palpable fact.

Most religions, including Christianity, Islam, Judaism and all the others, no matter the motivations, indoctrinate people in the same or a similar way.

Why else would we believe such stories and accept such sectarian doctrines with so much influence upon our lives if we were not brainwashed from so early an age that most of us could not even remember when it all began?

Do not blame God.

Don't even blame those men that began most of the religions. I believe their intentions were good. Perhaps they attempted to civilise mankind and make people into something better than they are; one can only speculate.

Through history, it is my firm belief, that the original concept of most religions has been altered or lost completely.

Keep in mind, despite all of them purporting to believe in God, every religion is different and in some cases willing to massacre all none-believers.

f. Then why do religions hold so much sway over our lives?

I believe the answer to the above question is a simple one, if somewhat controversial, distasteful and really rather sad: it is a combination of mass human insecurity and protracted brainwashing – some would call it nothing more than education – but like so much of indigenous cultures, brainwashing is a far more accurate description.

That is why religion has such a grip on the world; it is ingrained in our way of life.

Consider Britain, sometimes described as the mother of democracy and one of the truly free countries of the world.

Nonetheless, Britain supports a totalitarian system that is forced upon every citizen, no matter what the wishes of any individuals might be. If anyone fails to comply with this dictatorial edict they will be subjected to the full negative force of the law. What is this forced system?

Education!

Britain is a democracy and more free than most countries. But like it or not, from the age of five years, we are subject to the enforced brainwashing dictated by the state.

An overstatement you may think. Twisting the truth to suit an extreme argument you might declare. Well, to some extent, I agree.

After all, everyone needs and deserves a good education. But like it or not, that is when religious brainwashing usually begins.

Now take my, somewhat jaded description, and apply it to countries where populations are not encouraged to think for themselves – where ignorance and dictatorships really exist.

Is it any wonder that some people can be convinced that blowing themselves up in the name of their faith is the right thing to do?

Ending religion would be totally unthinkable for the majority of human beings, so ingrained has it become.

Facing the world without some kind of faith – preferably mystical – would be too much for the majority of human insecurities and tribalistic leanings to endure.

The rag that we chewed as a child – the dolly, or some other cuddly object – they were replaced by religion and culture as we matured and our insecurities grew with us. But those religions began to take hold long before the other comforts were discarded.

Perhaps it would be best to end this chapter with a proposition other than my own.

The much respected and campaigning Archbishop of Canterbury William Temple (1881 – 1944) stated:

"It is a great mistake to suppose that God is only, or even chiefly, concerned with religion."

~

4

Race & Culture

Since the beginning of recorded history there have been differing cultures – but it wasn't always like that.

It is a generally accepted theory that homo-sapiens first appeared in a small group on the continent now known as Africa. Like a mighty oak tree develops from a small acorn, so humanity grew.

In the dim past, tribal divergence gave birth to varying languages. As humans multiplied and spread across the world so genetic variations and in-breeding produced, what we call, different races.

Like dogs, selective breeding fashioned everything from a poodle to a pit-bull terrier, so geographically isolated humans developed differing features and skin colours, but dogs are still dogs.

- There is only one race and that is the human race.

- When you scrape away the basic similarities, stereotypical statements, and localised cultural desires for a tribal sameness – usually born of insecurities – every human being is unique and different.

- If there were no cultural differences, there would be no racism.

- There will always be prejudices – or to put it another way, likes and dislikes.

I have had the good fortune to travel over a large part of this world. Even to the equatorial parts of Africa. I have never seen a black man. They are very dark brown in that part of Central Africa, but definitely not black.

By the same token, I have only ever seen one man that I could truly describe as white.

Alone and suffering some kind of mental agony, that poor soul slashed both his wrists and then kept the wounds open by putting his arms nearly elbow deep into a well-balanced bucket of warm water. Practically all the blood had drained from his body by the time he was discovered and he had, to all intents and purposes, turned white.

Those of us who are not varying shades of brown are usually a beige/pink with a few brown spots depending on age and good summers.

- The terms 'Black Man' and 'White Man' are political, discordant, based on perverse cultural diversity, negative historical record, physical inaccuracies and are utterly ridiculous.

- There are beautiful people of every shade of colour in terms of both looks and personality, just as there are ugly ones. It really is the same the whole world over. That is an evidential fact.

Colour or facial characteristics have very little to do with the person within. It is cultures and nationalistic tribalism that have created the real differences.

Most of those differences are a tribalistic habit, born of parochial custom and practice, within guarded borders, combined with a suspicious atmosphere of distrust and insecurity.

Those insecurities are further fed by religious teaching and educational brainwashing – virtually from the cradle.

England is a fine example (if the word 'fine' can ever be used in such a depreciating way) of the tribalism that still causes cultural diversity and confrontations today.

Forget immigrants or skin tones for a moment. You do not need a different coloured skin or a sectarian religion to find antagonism and destructive separatism in England.

Simply travel from the south to the north – or even from one West-Midlands village to another. See how the accents vary; observe the deliberately constructed differences which are in place.

Imagine a conversation between natives of London, Birmingham, Newcastle-Upon-Tyne, Liverpool and someone from a small village just outside Penzance.

If they managed to understand each other (and that is very hard to imagine) it would be difficult to believe they all came from the same small country and, at most, only lived a couple of hundred miles or so apart.

Now imagine the same exercise with an Englishman, a German, an Iranian, an Israeli, a North-Korean and an American.

Is it any wonder the world is such a volatile place?

The one bright thought to consider about England is, despite the regional or even village differences, the vast majority will all proudly state that they are English, especially if challenged by outside adversity.

That position is by no means unique and we will return to the implications of a uniting situation in other chapters; but the inference is that when threatened, we are able to put aside our petty contrived differences.

- The greater the threat to a community, country, or part of the world, the greater the unity between those threatened people.

- The natural instinct, bred from necessity, which caused homo-sapiens to first herd, then tribe, has bastardised into a destructive national parochialism that flourishes throughout the world. It must be changed.

- We are all uniquely different, but those singular physical and personality variations do not matter. We are one race – all the same – all human beings.

- If the world's population is to survive and flourish beyond the next century we must all strive for cultural sameness, not divisive difference – one race, one universal language.

- Communication, taken to the most sophisticated degree, where differences are hardly a noticed consideration – other than personal self-individuality – is the uniting force that can bring the world together.

- We must all share one vision and recognise that we do face an overwhelming threat greater than any peoples of the world has ever faced before.

- In order to meet that threat, universally shared objectives and ideals must become human ideology from the cradle to the grave.

- Individual likes and dislikes should always be nurtured and respected, but never to a degree where they can bring disharmony to a shared world culture.

- The world's population ought to be free to self-determine, but only as individuals. Where that self-determination has a harmful or extreme influence, it must be controlled and nullified.

The so called 'politically correct' element of many western societies appear to be the people who have significant influence at this time (2013) but I suggest that their policies of racial and cultural tolerance are totally wrong.

Praising and accepting mass tribalistic difference will only ever create divisions between factions of society.

Difference between individuals does not matter.

We are all different and that variation makes us tolerable, interesting and often attractive to each other, despite obvious personality clashes that naturally occur.

Difference does not need to gain anymore attention or importance simply because it is amplified and epitomised by those seeking separatism.

Neither should diversity be glorified by pacifistic appeasers.

It is humanity's sameness that we need to encourage and admire.

- Culture is nothing more than a custom and practice that a group decide to follow, usually started at the behest of one highly motivated, commanding and persuasive character.

- Another inexorable truth is that, due to the vast insecurities of human beings, nearly everyone feels they must belong to something.

Belonging to something might be a community. I live in the West-Midlands of England, but that was not where I originally came from.

I was born just outside London in the county of Kent. I lived there for the first 22 years of my life. Those early years resulted in me having a pronounced urban south-eastern accent.

Since living in the Midlands, I have been called a 'mouthy southy' (not that far from the truth), a 'southern cockney' (is there any other kind?) and, believe it or not, a 'foreigner'.

It should be noted that the West-Midlands is a fairly cosmopolitan area of England.

After nearly 30 years, I am accepted, but mostly because of recognition, I am still that cockney chap, thanks to my accent.

The kind of banter I and millions of other people have been subjected to is caused by cultural tribalism.

In some parts of Great Britain, they really do detest the people from the next village – and that's even before they consider which football team they support!

Such, usually harmless, behaviour is however damagingly divisive when fed by third parties.

Political correctness law (which is probably the most divisive legislation ever formulated) suddenly ensures banter becomes much more, especially in the hands of the manipulative and unscrupulous.

Banter is only offensive when clearly used with insulting tones, or conversely, when someone wishes to be offended.

The fact that I am not a cockney but from Kent (cockneys are Londoners born within the sound of Bow Bells), or that someone of African origin has not got a black skin but a brown one, does not matter.

Often our perceived differences will be negatively described to let us know in very clear terms that we do not belong and are not part of the local tribe.

Political and religious interference feeds tribalism, no matter what the ideals or motivations.

The politicisation of thoughtless or derogatory remarks (which might, or might not, have had root within perceived ethnic origins or culture) probably started out with the best of ideals and purpose, but it has become the proverbial road to hell paved with good intentions.

All anti-racism laws have fostered is cultural divisiveness – tribalism instead of integration.

You cannot have schools preaching culturalistic nationalism and Christianity (or any other sectarian religion) on the one hand and then expect all the people with so many fundamental differences to come together as one harmonious populace; no matter how nationalistically persuaded they may be.

Political correctness has led to aging members of society throughout the western world feeling disenfranchised (younger indigenous populations sometimes believe they actually owe ethnic minorities something for the professed wrongs of past generations) and that legislation has presided over a general deterioration of personal freedoms for all ages.

The law may have driven cultural dislikes underground, but the thoughts are still there among the differing tribes, bubbling away under the surface, ready to explode in bouts of negative sectarianism when perceived slights have been suffered, standards of living have dropped, or someone wants an excuse to start trouble for their own perverse gratification.

If someone chooses to live in a certain area of the world then that person must expect to fit in with that region's way of life.

If the new conditions are unacceptable, then they should go back to where they came from and be happy with the way of life in that place instead.

However, the whole human race must accept that doctrinaire 'ways of life' are far out of proportion to the system this world's population must strive to achieve.

The main point to be remembered is that tribalism is a part of our fundamental custom and practice, since human time began – a natural instinct.

It would be almost impossible to remove tribalism from our fundamental being. Instead that instinct must be broadened, supported and sustained to a point where there is only one tribe, one race and one culture.

Tribalism was forced on mankind in order to survive. The day to day risks for early man ensured that nobody could endure alone for very long.

Those early necessities provided the seeds that grew the first insecurities that still haunt people today.

The problems the human species has already begun to face (and will become more frighteningly apparent in only a few short years) will require one tribe, united – if we are to stand any chance of enduring.

- If a change is ever to be brought about, it must be fundamental and managed by the governments of the world's major countries. Again, not a unique event – if the threat is considered great enough.

History teaches us that during the second world war (1939 – 1946) the United States, Russia, Canada, Australia, New Zealand, India and many more European, Asian and African countries came together to meet a threat to their freedom.

Nature shows us that most species will unite to face common adversity. However, take away that common negative purpose and our petty insecurities, likes and dislikes, take over.

Rather like mindless sheep, we become managed by narcissistic, amoral leaders who constantly over-estimate their collective abilities and individual intelligence.

Those leaders continually strive for unnecessary change, reinventing the metaphoric wheel again and again so they can egotistically declare, 'am I not clever? Look what I did!'

- We are only limited by boundaries erected by the smallness of our minds.

~

From the moment a human is born, cultural indoctrination begins. No matter how distasteful the term sounds, what I am describing is cultural and religious brainwashing. That negative, forced indoctrination is fed and encouraged by every nation on Earth.

- Flag waving nationalism is continually supported at every level of human existence and so are the antagonisms that accompany it.

- The mystic reverence subscribed to religions by almost every national government aids culturism and separatism.

Throughout the world people learn at a very young age that they are either Christians, Muslims, Buddhists, Sikhs, Jews or Hindus, and so forth.

Then, depending on the politics that accompany all the out-dated far-fetched sects, populations are brainwashed into accepting those ridiculously ritualised faiths as if they had just been handed down from above and witnessed by millions.

Thus divisive cultures are born and nurtured to a point where the people of Earth are currently prevented from ever coming together as one race.

It's not the fact that all those differing religions exist, although I do absolutely believe that today's world would be a far better place without them, it is the level of importance granted to religion that creates many of the major negative issues that so often end in acts of violence, or even wars.

Nearly all the culturally-affected religions have their own 'uniforms' to aid that tribalistic sense of belonging. The 'uniforms' vary in size and expressiveness depending on the degree of fanaticism.

Most Christians go no further than a cross and chain, although it is very rare to see a Catholic woman without some kind of head covering in church.

Minority sects such as the Amish and Quakers can be observed in their own traditional dress styles that scream out, 'I'm different to you and wish to be treated as such.' The one good thing about them is that their beliefs and way of life is very benign.

Male Sikhs usually insist on turbans (for their uncut hair) they must wear a dagger, a bracelet, a comb and cotton underpants, collectively (with the hair) known as the five Ks. Words fail me; I was once castigated for refusing to walk under a ladder!

Male Jews have skull caps (yarmulke) and prayer shawls (talits). Many orthodox Jews wear Homburgs complete with hairstyles that resemble Rastafarian dreadlocks. And to think, back in the early 60s, my Jewish uncle once told me I looked ridiculous with half a jar of Brilcream in my hair.

Male Muslims favour long beards (often without moustaches) and Middle-Eastern or Central Asian clothes, while the women regularly wear varying versions of the Hijab right up to the extreme complete concealment of a Burka.

Hindus appear to mainly favour Asian styles of dress, which is probably as much a cultural rather than religious statement.

Collectively, the tribalistic dress of those religions often look out of place and eccentric to the point of bordering on the ridiculous given the weather they were originally designed for and the places where the practitioners may now live.

All the 'uniforms' and their cultural displays are by no means unique.

Since the first army invaded another territory right up to modern times, if you want to give the dominating, oppressing or fanatical group a visible sense of identity and belonging, put them in a uniform.

Nazi Germany managed to take perfectly normal human beings (with all the caring humanities and empathies enjoyed by most peaceful peoples) and brainwash a controlling uniformed populace numbering hundreds of thousands. They were collectively turned into murderous abominations that heartlessly slaughtered millions with a cold sadism that defies all logical reason.

The brainwashing that young minds are subjected to by Islamic extremists, like Hitler's Germany, is an equally polished 'fine-art' of control.

How many sane intelligent people could you persuade to strap a bomb to themselves and then set it off while attempting to murder as many innocent men, women and children as possible?

Paradoxically, like the brainwashing skills of Adolf Hitler, Islamic, and other cultural extremists of the 21st century, actually point the way for the betterment and future security of the human race; but more in-depth examinations of that irony will follow later.

One way or another, all humans subscribe to some form of culturalism/tribalism that has been brainwashed into them, usually from birth.

All of those practices are outdated rubbish and should be actively discouraged by the world's governments.

Rather like smoking, I suspect the official view is there would be too much confrontation and negative financial implications were such powerful organisations to be essentially challenged.

- If humankind is to have a long-term potential, we must move towards one culture and the acceptance that we are all one race.

The rights of the individual must be maintained. Remember, your version of God may well not be another's, but all versions should be respected and the facets of the inherent culture, because nobody knows the answers to life's biggest questions and anyone who states that they do is either a brainwashed fool or a liar.

But those individual rights must be contextualised.

No racial, cultural or religious beliefs should ever be allowed to damage the above bullet pointed proposition.

~

5

Change & the reasons for it

Change is an absolute certainty, like birth and death. There are no other certainties in life. Everything else is a probability or a possibility.

Change is as immutable as the universe itself; it is more a certainty than birth and death.

But consider; how do the three certainties of existence fit with the first of my three assertions of absolute fact in the first chapter?

To remind you:-

When contemplating any aspect of existence, the known universe, or infinity; there will always be an exception to any fact discovered, no matter how simple the fact, or how overwhelming the evidence may be supporting the fact. Nothing is ever accurately covered by one sweeping statement. No fact can ever be accepted without the reservation that all things are subject to incremental change, which by definition creates exception.

The answer is simple. There can be an exception to the immutable fact of birth, death and change.

Change can alter birth and death by ensuring they no longer exist. And that is precisely the philosophy I am expounding – an attempt to address such a cataclysmic finality.

Change is the only immutable fact that will continue after the human race and all other life on Earth (or anywhere else for that matter) ceases to exist.

Maybe there will come a time when change no longer exists either, but that, like so many intellectualised postulations, is a thought too far.

The essential point to grasp is just how important change will always be to humankind. Yet, how little most people understand about the mechanics of change…

- If we do not manipulate change then it will surely manipulate us.

- There are only four kinds of change.

I. Incremental Change – an alteration that occurs over a protracted period – slowly. Most people hardly notice it happening until that change is already successfully established.

II. Paradigm Change – an alteration that requires a new concept and a different way of thinking; a quantum shift from whatever went before.

III. Pendulum Change – a change not implemented or supported properly; something altered that reverts back to the way it was.

IV. Change by Exception – a heading with two related meanings. Alterations that occur without plan or immediate explanation; the exception to the rule. Or, a change achieved by an individual who is deemed to be exceptional or an exception.

Those four types of change are more fully described in a book entitled 'Managing Management' (ASIN: B009PKDFMQ) but do be assured, every change you can think of, fits one of those four headings.

Manipulating change means an idea must be devised and accepted (the paradigm) then the resources must be allocated to allow the change to take place.

Resources are not simply manpower and money; they must contain detailed plans for every stage of the change and contingences to support, monitor and keep the change on-track, otherwise a pendulum will be the result.

The natural resistance that people have for any alteration and the expected inertia, which results from that conscious or unconscious resistance, suggests that support at all stages of a paradigm transformation must be enthusiastic, continual and will always be imperative if a protracted incremental change is finally to be achieved.

Remember, the greater the paradigm, the more chance of a pendulum.

- Successful incremental alteration (resulting from a paradigm concept) on a worldwide scale should be expected to take decades, or even centuries.

Having mentioned the natural resistance that people have against changes does perhaps require some small explanation.

There are, in fact a plethora of reasons, some as individual as the people concerned.

Nonetheless, there are two major causes that nearly always apply and generally contribute to the most mass resistance.

1. A lack of clear visual pay value for the people involved with, or a part of, the change. (Sometimes quite wrongly described as motivation. Visual pay value can be the motivation, but motivation can never be, by itself, visual pay value, which is far more self-interested and fundamental to any person.) If people do not feel they are a part of any alteration, or there is something significant in the change for them, the probability that they will resist it is only one very small step down from the three certainties of life.

2. Change usually means being required to leave the security of our comfort zone – to think in new ways and accept new practices and systems. Human insecurities ensure that, throughout our lives, the vast majority of us strive to achieve habits that are functional and continuous – a regular routine, the velvet lined rut – places of familiarity that make us feel safe and help us manage all our insecurities.

After having condemned the world's egotistical and insecure politicians and leaders for making changes for their own arrogant and avaricious reasons, I feel it only correct to justify the massive incremental adjustments recommended by me in the next chapter.

Having criticised everyone who narcissistically makes an alteration for 'changes' sake, it is important to validate something that could potentially alter the lives of so many people.

Perhaps also, the negativity of the first few chapters needs more justification as well.

Remember how I have condemned anyone who accepts something fundamental and significant without seeking some evidential substantiation?

Well, here is my rationale…

~

We live on an unstable planet in a volatile universe. It goes almost without saying, we wish that existence to continue for the long term, no matter how we might deny it to ourselves, it is a natural instinct.

A selfish or blasé statement such as, 'I don't care what happens when I'm gone,' or, 'we're all going to be finished soon, what does it matter?' are the words of a selfish, ignorant minority.

Humans collectively fight for life the same as every other living species.

But this wish for continued existence is not just for the length of our lifetimes. For all of us who are parents, we would wish harmonious continuation to persist for our children – our grandchildren, their children, and so on.

Whoever found a greater love or reason to live than having the privilege of watching children grow?

Who could ever grudge them life and the chance of enjoying the same understanding we have experienced?

However, clear unmistakeable evidence, suggests their days are numbered. It is almost impossible for the world to continue and progress successfully if we carry on as we are. There are many negative factors that we need to overcome, but the most critical are:-

a) A burgeoning world population.

b) The Earth's apparently declining natural resources.

c) Our vulnerability to the whims of nature.

d) The corrupt, divisive and short term policies produced and implemented by the majority of world governments.

e) The lack of importance and investment granted to scientific research.

f) The continuing acceptance of divisive cultural extremism and the adverse effects of a misdirected education system.

a*) The world's population grows larger year by year; increasing despite wars, disease, starvation and natural disaster.

Rather like a cancer, if Earth's human population continues to grow, chances are, it will destroy the body it inhabits.

Mathematically speaking, it is impossible not to start deteriorating as a world civilisation in less than another two centuries.

Do the sums yourselves, perhaps with only the inhabitants of China at first. Then add India and Africa.

Note the yearly population increases, then use that increasing percentage for your projections. Like a snowball down a mountain – I've never seen one grow smaller.

Observe the suffering some areas of our world already endure when it comes to placing food in the mouths of the young. You cannot make a suit of clothes for a large man if you only have enough material for a small one.

Even in countries such as Britain, which enjoys restrained population growth, house building has been an almost continuous fact since 1945.

In the past, our expansionistic desires and population necessities explored and then colonised areas of the world where hardly any other humans dwelt.

However, our planet is now so overcrowded that only war, mass-genocide, natural pandemic or slow starvation temper the continual population increase. But such tragedies only slow that augmentation briefly; what a condemnation those facts are of our so called, civilised, forward thinking, humane society.

We are what we are. Our needs will not change in the foreseeable future. Humanity requires more room and more resources.

Yet there is the vastness of our solar system and beyond to discover and inhabit.

In the 1950s and 60s, there was a, virtually world-wide, excitement and positive feeling as humankind looked towards the stars.

Many spacecraft flights and eventual moon landings fuelled the imagination of millions. Sadly, it all turned out to be nothing more than egotistical posturing between two world super powers. There appears to have been no higher ideals or forward thinking among the leaders of those two countries. No plans for securing the future prospects of our race were in their minds.

By almost unwritten mutual agreement, nearly all major space programmes were scaled back. Cost was deemed far too high. Once again the moneymen forced the issue with tragically negative results.

If only there had been a written agreement between those super powers and other influential countries of the world to pool resources and jointly continue space exploration.

Where might we have been by now?

Surely profit and success should be measured by humankind's flourishing progression? Not by market-force driven fiscal gains that benefit only a few multi-millionaires.

Conversely, perhaps the most important point to consider in our topsy-turvy general unpredictability is also the most idealistically welcome.

History suggests that humankind actually is a continually altering and developing dynamic. We seemingly stagger forward, through great strife and inhumanities, to ostensibly emerge just a little better and an almost immeasurable fraction wiser.

Our international targets appear to grow more humane. While among a sea often filled with waves of corruption, sleaze and other amoral behaviour, somehow, empathy for each other does seem to increase.

Would we not all wish that process to be less painful and protracted? And perhaps more planned and directed?

From an examination of humanity's past, it would appear not unreasonable to predict that we might be, very slowly, changing into something better than we were, or are now.

Yet time is becoming a critical factor.

No matter how humanity might slowly advance, we cannot move forward if we destroy the environment humans are currently progressing from; all the while lacking the ability of migrating towards pastures new.

~

b*)   Our planet's resources are being used up at alarming rates.

Those priceless natural commodities are eaten away by ever more demand from an increasing population and technology, designed almost totally for the consumer plus the greed of short term profit.

Many consumer gadgets have little more than a five year lifetime.

The waste from such cynical voracity – all for continually increasing returns, coupled with a worldwide worship of market-place economics, together with that burgeoning population – will ensure that the finite raw materials our planet supplies have a very limited life.

Yet there are moons and worlds within our solar system which rudimentary examinations show contain vast resources.

~

c*)   Little encouragement is given for science (unless it is driven by the thought of profit for the private sector) to develop new resources that might be plentiful and cheap.

Earth grows ever more volatile as climate change continues. Whether or not that alteration is a natural incremental progression, or caused by humankind, really does not matter. The important fact is, it's happening.

Science is not universally encouraged to find preventative solutions and provide contingency plans for the planetary changes, but only to supply explanations.

We must learn to control our environment.

I do not mean to imply we should strive for bright sunshine all day and rain between two and four in the morning – although perhaps that would be no bad thing. I mean having the abilities to predict an earthquake and minimise its effects. See the beginnings of hurricanes and dispel them before they wreak havoc. Control water flow before it floods properties and cultivated land.

Just as volatile and infinitely more dangerous are the uncertainties of our solar system.

Our star – the sun – is a very unstable body. Day by day it consumes itself at a tremendous rate.

Predictably, the sun should continue to shine for thousands of years yet. Its life might be a long one, but one day it will end, we have no way of knowing when, only speculation.

The sun's volatility causes it to excrete, among other things, deadly solar winds. Were it not for our planet's well-developed magnetic field (known, for the purpose of deflecting solar winds, as the 'Lorentz force' and/or magnetosphere) which deflects the solar wind around the Earth, all life (as we know it) would probably cease to exist.

Speculation suggests Mars once had a magnetosphere, almost certainly held water and possibly supported life. Mars has not got a 'Lorentz force' now and appears to be a dead sterile world.

Nobody really knows, but Mars may well be a very graphic predictor of Earth's natural progression.

What we do know is that we have no way of controlling anything on a solar system-wide scale.

There are no contingency plans for artificially controlling our environment on a planetary-wide scale.

The unpredictability of space-born meteors could cause a cataclysmic event on Earth and set our progression back a thousand years, or even destroy us completely.

We know that our planet has been struck many times throughout its long history by objects from space. We can only speculate about what devastating changes those strikes caused. Our devices for spotting potential dangers from space are crude and wholly inadequate.

Our chances of stopping, or deflecting, a large meteor on a collision course with Earth are virtually none.

Humanity cannot continually remain with its metaphoric head in the sand and hope a catastrophe that could end our world will never happen. The probability of a disaster from space grows with every passing decade. History seems to indicate that a crude time-related pattern does exist regarding the ebb and flow of meteors journeying within our solar system.

We must safeguard and nurture our existence.

Like trusting naïve children, for far too long, we have wrongly assumed humanity's existence is infinite and depends on the benevolence of some guardian angel or spiritual deity. Maybe it does, but I have not seen any rational evidence to convince me that something so important should be left to something so tenuous, at best.

Unfortunately, there is little visual pay value in preparing for a disaster that – except in science fiction movies – hardly anyone has ever heard of, leave alone witnessed.

Rather like someone told to give up smoking…

"It will kill you in a few years if you continue with your forty-a-day habit."

"But I feel fine; it's obviously not harming me, and the nicotine (which is the person's real visual pay value) makes me feel good. So why should I stop?"

It's a question of everything being alright at the moment and there are dozens of other issues with far more pressing importance.

Let me give you another analogy.

The smoker develops lung cancer. She is told there's a slim chance for her life to continue – an operation in two weeks time – but she must give up smoking immediately. The pain in her chest gets a little worse every day. Her visual pay value just suddenly changed. What do you think she will do?

Perhaps people wouldn't wait so long to make important decisions if they forgot their insecurities, emotions and selfish short-term goals, just simply used their common-sense, considered all the evidential facts – then thought about the children.

~

d-e*)   Many politicians and governments throughout the world are corrupt and incompetent. Very few, if any, have any real long-term vision. Their collective Gods are a mixture of money, power, toadying to big business and their own ambition.

Frequently, politicians are not even their own masters. Should they have forward-thinking policies, more often than not, they will be quashed by the faceless moneymen and the influence that those dubious people wield; either that, or on rare occasions, the usually wrongly perceived, media driven, wishes of voters sway some of them – around election time.

Just because someone was clever enough to gain a first-class degree in anthropology at university, it does not qualify them to run a country's health service; yet we all know variations on such an example are not uncommon.

So it is with scientific development.

More often than not, the politicians in charge of scientific research and advancement haven't got the faintest idea what they are doing and lack the guidance of clear direction or long-term objectives.

It is a familiar practice that the financing of science usually depends on the inadequate pennies from universities and the market-economy driven purse strings of private enterprise.

The politicians will normally only find significant money if they wish to bomb the living daylights out of an enemy with some new all-singing and dancing weapon.

Fortunately, the majority of scientists are among the most dedicated and selfless people in the world. They are usually motivated by the thought of actually doing something worthwhile rather than simply making a profit.

However, important research and development should not need to rely on such tenuous planning and ill-financed effort.

Without science, the human race will not last as long as the dinosaur.

- Sooner or later, all our lives depend on the skill of scientists.

Our existence has been reliant on science since humans first crawled from caves.

If we are to survive for the long-term future, then science will be the main reason for that continued successful existence. There is no other better proven method.

My God only helps those who help themselves. Unless you honestly know otherwise, I suggest that, in this regard, your version of God is probably the same.

~

f*) The cultures on Earth feed separatism and racial disharmony.

The sycophantic policies towards extremist cultures dictated by many western governments do nothing but provide a home and breeding ground for continuing culture-driven terrorism. Those same policies repeatedly feed the extremist elements of all factions.

How many atrocities have been committed in the Western World by so-called home-grown terrorists?

Worse still are the effects on education.

Within the United Kingdom there are Islamic, Sikh and Jewish schools that openly teach a different culture to that of the British majority.

Not much better are the Christian schools, with their seemingly compassionate approach, they nevertheless lay the seeds for a separatism that has nothing to do with the realities of life – only the insecurities.

Education in Britain generally is failing society.

There is a massive skills gap (especially in the sciences) within most practical areas.

Obscure academic subjects consume far too many scholastic resources.

Numerous teachers and lecturers exist in a middle-class cosseted world. Sometimes they have had little to do with the day-to-day realities that face much of humankind.

On a worldwide basis, education lacks cohesive direction.

Frequently manipulated by dictatorial national governance, school systems continually give birth to new generations of tribalism, rather than seeking to unite the planet's population.

Some cultures deliberately exclude women from the education system completely. Others use it as a weapon to brainwash young minds into being compliant puppets often incapable of thinking clearly for themselves.

The evidence does seem both overwhelming and patently obvious: we must change.

Our development is not going fast enough to cope successfully with the threats to our long-term continued existence.

- Humanity needs unity on a worldwide scale.

- Humanity needs more space to grow.

- Humanity needs a greater supply of resources without the crippling burden of artificial market-force expense.

- We need structured and fully resourced technological advancement that supports our growth and future assets; not the currently prioritised continuing research for yet another smart-phone, entertainment system or similar unimportant but nice-to-have high profit commodities.

The next chapters describe the philosophical structures and systems which could form the basis for incremental changes that would ensure humankind has a more secured future – you decide!

6

A Structure for Change

We must change. The evidence is irrefutable. If we continue the way we are now, the human race will be doomed to extinction within a measurable time-span.

"We have got to use science as a prioritised necessity. Ways must be found to control and protect our environment.

Over a protracted period of many years, new technologies should be created to enable the colonisation of our solar system and beyond.

Huge space stations, comprising of several square miles, must be built in space. Capable of journeying for many years across the vast emptiness in search of

*new stars, those space stations must be the first crude
stepping stones that will see human beings populate
the galaxy.*

*Such actions will ensure the continuation of the
human race and supply the population of Earth with a
shared, positive, long term vision."*
Carl Sagan (1934 – 1996).

Excerpt from a speech made by Professor Sagan to the
American Association for the Advancement of Science.
For what it's worth, I absolutely agree with him.

- Expansionism on a planetary, then galactic scale is the
  only constructive conclusion for an ever increasing
  world population.

- Planetary and galactic colonisation can only succeed if
  the people of the Earth are united in that common
  cause.

Spelt out above is what should be the long-term dream,
the plan for a continuing future. If it isn't how we visualise
the future then we are not going to have one.

How such a project is financed will be dealt with in the
next chapter. For now it is the concept of a United World
that is most important to consider. That and accepting
human existence must have an identified shared direction;
at the moment, it hasn't got one, shared or otherwise.

- The world must be united – one official language that
  everyone understands.

- Only a united world with agreed long term objectives will guarantee the best possible chance for continued human existence.

As with finance, the details and the system particulars for successful change will be discussed later. For now, the overall political structure for a different world needs recording.

Before ways of achieving a journey are identified it is perhaps wise to have a detailed vision of a common sense destination, one that arguably, could begin tomorrow – something that simple and understandable.

~

If nothing else, one clear fact should have emerged from the previous five chapters. The human race is an incredible paradox; it contradicts itself upon nearly every major issue.

Take a single glaring example.

On the one hand, you have an animal that always longs to be free and self determine – singularly and collectively – even willing to die for the principle.

On the other hand, you have a creature that really is rather poor at being free and collectively, constantly lacks the skills required to self-determine successfully.

So that leads to another paradox.

How does one ensure that people feel that they live in a free world, while at the same time ensuring that the future is prescribed so that it is not a failure?

The answer is really rather simple, a global culture of ingrained structure and system.

Remember, our insecurities ensure that the vast majority of humanity seeks routine and predictable practice as a way of life.

We tend to measure success as an individual achievement. Even when there are teams involved, the media, and usually society in general, will look for the one or two exceptional individuals that perhaps, made that positive difference.

In the western world we have an amazing 'soft spot' for the entrepreneur or the exception – especially if this is a chap or lady with a nice smile and winning oratory. The mere fact that when he or she drops down dead there might well follow utter confusion and a rapidly failing fiscal empire, or even worse, a national loss of direction, is a truth that usually gets mislaid.

Then there are the insecure managers who are allowed too much entrepreneurial scope. Such managers introduce new ways of working when they take over and continually reinvent the wheel.

Irrespective of what they might state, the main reasons executives act as they do are twofold:

Their egos require they change for changes sake so that they can point to something and declare they did it. Then their insecurities demand they justify their professional existence.

- Very few people are capable of managing anything successfully over a protracted period without their authority and practice being underpinned by structure and system.

- Decade after decade of success never depends on an individual. It always depends upon the successful mandatory structure and systems put in place.

One of the most successful structures I can think of is the McDonalds food restaurants.

I have been in a McDonalds on four continents. Were it not for the differences in language and currency, I would never have known where I was; it could have been London, New York, Mauritius or Kula-Lumpur. The premises outer façade, the internal decoration, food and drink, uniforms and systems of working, were all the same – worldwide and wholly successful.

Irrespective of how you feel about fast-food chains, or other completely systemised organisations, no one can deny their amazing consistency and success over protracted periods (McDonalds started in 1940) while still maintaining the ability for implementing swift paradigm change if circumstances require.

Their management (both senior and middle) alters quite regularly, with hardly anyone noticing. Those managers are paid for supporting and maintaining the system; not tearing it down and rebuilding it in their own image.

If you think about it, countries should be the same as a systemised organisation. More often than not they operate similarly to a business and we all know what condition they get into if some other contradictory system – or no system at all – starts to dictate.

How many times have we seen perfectly successful organisations harmed, or publicly-owned utilities sold off for no more than dogmatic political whim? Usually a caprice of just one or two people.

Corruption has the scope to flourish under unconstrained entrepreneurialism.

It is far more difficult for mal-practice to thrive with identifiable procedures within a mandatory structure.

~

Britain is often credited with being the mother of parliaments. Or in other words, our system of democratic government has been adopted in many countries.

Wherever democracy exists, people feel free.

- The right to vote is one of the greatest freedoms enjoyed and supports the mass proposition of liberty and self-determination.

The ability to throw out one government (local or national) and replace it with another at the ballot box has stopped many a revolution and mass civil disorder before it really takes hold.

Or in other words, Britain may be responsible for dedicating the best principles of governmental system and structure to the world – but that system needs to be far more prescriptive for worldwide use.

The other important segment of perceived freedom is the right to express an opinion.

Free speech is the safety valve on the pressure cooker of public emotion.

Being able to say what you like (within the rule of acceptable laws of libel) is the other commodity that makes people feel they are free.

- Free speech and the right to vote for who governs us are the two founding necessities of any structure for world governance.

The philosophical argument about what true freedom is has some status in academic thought (true freedom is only in the mind – only when you have more money than you know what to do with can you be really free – only in dreams are you completely liberated – the only true freedom is death…) but such concepts will always be subjective and are really, rather irrelevant.

The point here for consideration is not what true freedom is, but what is collectively acceptable to the vast majority of human beings.

Given the fact that a considerable proportion of the world suffers dictatorship, or corrupt parodies of democracy, I doubt that many would put forward a serious argument against my two foundational necessities for a prescriptive world structure.

However, I accept that the thought of a world government is a concept too far for many people when first suggested. Such a paradigm change would initially meet more resistance than Adolf Hitler did when he attempted to subjugate most of Europe.

Such a quantum leap is too much to contemplate. It smacks at our national identity and pride. Everything a proud country holds dear would be swept away. To some extent that may be true, but national pride would still have its place.

Rather like culture and religion, nationalism would still exist, but contextualised. All of those practices have far too much negative influence on the world. That influence must be nullified.

Remember, all our current unconstructive traditions are achieving is the almost certainty of the human race ceasing to exist in an all-too foreseeable future.

~

Many Europeans might look at the, sometimes, fairly controversial, European Union (EU) and collectively shake their heads with despair. Perhaps upon many issues, I would agree with them.

The faults of the EU are numerous and full of nationalistic ambiguities; I've no wish to digress by listing any.

Nonetheless, it would be remiss of me not to point out one major blessing.

Since the EU existed, there has been a continual, unprecedented period of peace and some crude sense of a united purpose within its extensive bounds.

If nothing else, the EU is a massive indicator for the proposition that eventually, world peace and a cohesive sense of direction would almost certainly result from a United Earth.

Some might point to the North Atlantic Treaty Organisation (Nato) as the real peacekeeper in Europe. It may well have helped. No one could say otherwise.

But what about the other places outside the EU that Nato supposedly has influence? Not quite the same result, is it?

~

The concept envisaging some kind of United Earth is not as new as some may think.

The League of Nations (1919 – 1946) was a well-meaning attempt to minimise conflict and present a partially integrated world front. It was a largely toothless organisation that failed to achieve its key objective. Thanks mainly to Adolf Hitler, who was primarily responsible for all the Axis countries leaving the organisation.

After the Second World War ended (in 1946) the League was replaced by, the United Nations (UN).

The UN is a far more effective organisation, but even a casual observer can see it has glaring weaknesses and faults. Perhaps the biggest is the, often nationalistic, decisions made there.

Where petty alliances and cultural preferences are concerned, common sense usually flies out a New York, East River window.

Nonetheless, despite its faults, the UN and the earlier League were steps in the right direction. However, they go nowhere near far enough.

- A United World must have a clear mandatory structure and systems of practice to work within.

- A United World should be a democracy and have lucid long-term objectives.

- All objectives must be mandatory statutes and be recorded in a constitution.

- The World Government should have all the powers currently bestowed upon any democratically elected national government that exists today (2013) but the originating constitution must only be subject to amendment.

Although this chapter only really describes the overall structure for a world government, the above assertion is well made. For that philosophy describes one of the essential differences between the UN, past empires, the EU and what I am proposing.

A constitution – set of rules – charter of practice – call it what you will (I prefer constitution).

But, any constitution must be mandatory and enforceable by the world government and, perhaps more importantly, adhered to by that administration with the full enforcement of international law.

Just as constitutions are already accepted in many democratic countries throughout the Western World; only in such a way can a world government have legitimate direction and responsibility. With all the power that accompanies such accountable dictates.

- A constitution goes beyond the rule of law; it is the foundation from which fair and legitimate legislation springs.

- A constitution (with its accompanying amendments) becomes greater than the sum of a current government. It develops into the structure and guidance to govern by – the wisdom and experience of those that have gone before.

~

A proven workable structure, which already exists today, could easily be applied to the world.

The United States of America (USA – US) may not be everyone's favourite country. But forget politics, policies or even personalities for a minute.

Anyone who has toured extensively throughout the USA will know that each of the fifty states are, in many cases, as different as countries.

The population mix, law, geography, accent, customs and mode of dress often vary considerably from one state to another. They all have their own 'state' identity and are proud of it.

Each US state has its own 'government'. That governing body has elected representatives which form part of the national government.

But the USA has something else that really is rather unique.

Despite each state having so much autonomy – as much as some countries – US citizens have a collective national identity of which they are very proud. They might be Texans or from Vermont – a chalk and cheese existence – but at the end of the day, all are US Americans; first and foremost.

It is perhaps worth remembering that the United Kingdom would fit into the state of Texas nearly three times. Yet Texas is just one state of fifty.

According to which set of official figures you ascribe to, there are allegedly one hundred and ninety-six countries on Earth today.

Why not a United States of the World?

The system obviously works. The USA is a multi-cultural society that has an even stronger national identity; and it succeeds.

The USA is the most powerful nation on Earth; it has accomplished more in recent history, over a wide spectrum of achievement, than any other country.

Perhaps USA history is an indicator of what it takes to give birth to such a huge nation made of so many differing states. Despite many languages being spoken when first settled, it became obvious that only one official tongue was practical.

In over three hundred years, there has only been one major war between the states. That conflict was in the pursuit of freedom and democracy for all; or arguably, the enforcement of the USA's constitution.

The USA model is a tried and tested structure that could easily be applied on a world-wide basis. That model is also a perfect example of a successful incremental change.

The first 'United States' emerged during the eighteenth century (1770 – 1788) but it was not until the early twentieth century (1912) that all the mainland territories finally achieved statehood.

In the second part of the century (1958 – 1959) two more states were formed. One was as the result of a much earlier purchase of land (Alaska) from another country (Russia).

However, the second state of the fifties was the Hawaiian Islands; a group of atolls far removed from any continental mainland with arguably, an entirely differing race and culture. If that is not an indicator of how the USA's structure could work on a world-wide basis, I don't know what is!

The USA's structure and governmental systems are not perfect; but then, nothing on Earth created by humans comes close to flawlessness (except perhaps for music – remember, there is always an exception).

What the USA structure does provide is a tried and proven template for probably the most fundamental and positive change this world could ever make.

The structure shows the way to an achievable goal instead of a United World being nothing more than an intellectualised postulation.

Rather like the USA, a United World would be a very prolonged objective to achieve. Perhaps some countries would never become a part of such a union.

Isolationist states such as North Korea, Somalia and Myanmar would probably choose to remain as they are for the foreseeable future. Then there are those that love their own individual power or grip upon the populace but still purport to be a part of world organisations. I find it hard to imagine Russia, China or most of the Arab nations being founding countries of a United World.

It really does not matter.

If members of the EU (who already see the benefits of being united) the USA, Canada, Australia, New Zealand, Japan, other European countries and many of the world's smaller nations were members of a United World, one might well be surprised how quickly other influential countries would apply to join.

The hardest part for any enterprise of such magnitude is beginning.

It is always much easier for the powers that be to simply do nothing. Or better still, point to the few positive advancements being made by scientists and humanity in general.

And there are positive advancements being made – almost everyday. Sadly, raindrops of comfort in an ocean of pain.

~

7

Systems for Change,

Education & Funding.

If the structure is a house, then systems are the wiring, plumbing and everything else that makes the dwelling function. A simple equation everyone understands.

However, if you think about it, you'll realise that same equation of structure and system really applies to everything that has a function. Yet so many organisations try to manage without either.

- Systems, by their very nature are authoritative habits.

Humans are creatures of habit. Tasks become more recognisable when following a set routine; they are easier to perform and are usually completed with a higher degree of quality.

From a professional point of view, if everyone understands the systems and routines the job is made predictable, quality is simpler to assure and efficiency can be maximised.

Systems do not stop innovation or entrepreneurialism; they provide a firm base for the former and temper the excesses of the latter.

Although many working people dislike some aspects of the mundane predictability of professional routine, most would admit that the only replacement for systemisation is disorganised chaos.

Rather like change, people do resist imposed systems. Akin to any kind of imposition, fixed routine smacks at personal freedoms.

Care should always be taken whenever mandatory systemisation is introduced.

Obviously, much of the organisation for United World Governance would be put in place subject to the countries forming the original membership.

No matter how united the world might become, 'local' current aspirations and expectations of founding members would always have influence upon a final draft constitution. It would be unrealistic to ever think otherwise.

However, there are some things that I see as necessity from the beginning, if the dream is ever to be realised.

- A constitution must clearly state all the major procedural rules for a world government.

Procedural rules are not only guidelines that point the way to realising objectives. They provide the constraints to work within that only allow for focused efforts to succeed.

The following system examples I give are by no means complete or necessarily prescriptive, but they are tenets that I cannot imagine any democratic world government managing without.

- Elections ought to be held in constituent countries every five years.

- No elected World Government member should be permitted to serve more than two consecutive terms.

- World Government members should vote and elect a Head of State. That figurehead's only power above other members will be representational, holding a casting vote, and to call elections as constitutional time or circumstances dictate.

- Members ought to elect a Collator of Governance who will chair government sessions. The Chair will forgo the right to vote on all matters while in office, remaining non-executive and ideally, non-partisan.

- The Collator shall be responsible for order, discipline and verbatim records. The position will exist for a period no longer than the term of three governments.

It is very easy to become bogged down with tedious detail; therefore, although far from a complete panacea, the afore-mentioned procedures are designed to underpin a democracy and should provide some palpable safeguards for its long-term continuance.

However, for the sake of succinctness, I'll go no further with the detail for government administration.

An open press ensures free speech and should always be encouraged to act as a watch-dog upon political figures everywhere, while the internet ensures that autonomy subsists.

But perhaps what matters most of all, are the dedicated long-term policies that spring from the original constitutional foundations.

~

A United World would be a waste of time without long-term policies that provide and support overall purpose and direction. My final philosophy supplies some constitutional objectives that may ensure the basis for a more harmonious continuation of the human race.

Education

Education for all age-groups is the most vital part of any substantial change and its future success.

What can be achieved by good schooling should never be underestimated; but so far, it is arguably the evil fanatic that has taken education to its highest level of single-minded achievement.

History shows that dictators and terrorists have utilised educational systems to brainwash young people into becoming compliant tools.

Our school systems in the western world show we produce a culture that has multiple weaknesses and divisive consequences.

Diversity regarding cultures and religions are not subjects that require or deserve the level of importance that they currently enjoy, politically or educationally.

The human race must be united and that sameness as a race is what should be emphasized.

- Social and cultural instruction within schools throughout the world ought to shape young minds to accept one official language, one race and the need for united expansionism on an interplanetary scale.

- All religious instruction should be limited to a similar position of subjects such as art and crafts. Nice to know topics, but of little importance for the majority of people in the real world and eventually, just a matter of personal choice and practice – no more than that.

- Education must, first and foremost, concentrate on filling the skill gaps created by world governmental policy and those of associated industries.

- All faith based schools ought to be closed and replaced by specialisations in the sciences so that the establishment of meaningful scientific research is created earlier and on a wider basis.

- The political definitions of black and white races should cease. Children must be taught that skin colour and facial features have no more significance than the colour of eyes or hair – a matter of personal taste along with personality likes and dislikes.

State education is probably one of the most important parts of human development.

How we educate our young will largely decide the way a society, and arguably, humanity point-blank, will progress in the future.

At this moment in time, even in the western world among allied countries, our education systems have tremendous differences.

One of the first acts of a World Government should be to provide educational uniformity, with a fixed curriculum that supports government goals and objectives.

It should also be policy to offer education to the young from all non-aligned countries.

Brainwashing is usually seen as an extreme, or totalitarian, act. But like it or not, that's what education is.

People must feel free, but if they're not pointed in the right direction from the cradle, then for sure, many will find a wrong path at the hands of some predatorial fanatic or another.

Education is not just about reading, writing and arithmetic. It's about shaping young minds so they read what civilisation wants them to, write how humanity dictates and use the sums to solve the problems that a World Government and a scientifically motivated populace identifies.

If any of those children, in the fullness of time, decide those objectives are not what they want to do, then so be it.

The rights of the individual should always be respected.

People must be free to choose. However, most intelligent human beings usually seek to make an informed choice, which inevitably amounts to what detail is placed before them. That information should be credible and honest but nevertheless, strongly influenced by the United World's aims and objectives.

Finance

Sooner or later the realisms of life demand that any changes require some statement of funding, or they would be deemed unrealistic and pie-in-the-sky.

- I suggest funding and current fiscal expression is a false concept that, under its present connotation, should cease for the financing of a World Government and its business.

The majority of the world engages in trade within the market economy. Countries are assessed by what they produce, the services they provide, how much they earn and how much they spend. Their worth is also calculated in gold reserves, natural resources and private fiscal machinations upon the world's financial index systems.

All of that is false!

- The whole method of the current world economy is artificially created to produce a totally fictionalised fiscal reality. It is based on political practice, entrepreneurial cunning, greed, amoral tradition and dictatorial enforcement founded on tribalistic separatism.

Once-upon-a-time, a farmer grew crops and produced dairy products; but his wife wanted clothes for the children and furniture for the house. So the farmer found a tailor and a carpenter and traded some of his goods for theirs – thus the free market economy based on trade was born.

Contrary to what some people think, I'm not that old and I wasn't there, but back in the mists of history, which is when the market economy began, the farmer's produce swap, or something very similar, occurred – supply and demand was born.

On the whole, the system was a good one until the entire disorganised world and its governments became involved and complicated the issue; now it's just a largely unregulated massive car-crash that happens with increasing reliability – boom and bust!

Competition is preached in the western world as if it were sanctified. Yet just how bogus that method really is becomes exemplified when corrupt and incompetent practice results in countries running out of money.

The last world economic downturn (2009 – 2013) saw some countries all but declaring bankruptcy. They were then apparently assisted financially by other states.

The real truth was that populations from the insolvent nations would not accept further austere policies placed upon them by their governments. So money suddenly became available with ridiculous interest rates and vast numbers quoted that expediency soon allowed to be forgotten.

Yet more countries eased the financial burden of their populace by something imaginatively called 'quantitative easing'.

No matter how governments disguise that 'easing' system (buying 'government bonds' or artificial assets, which are usually no more than entries in a book or its computerised equivalent) it all means the same thing; printing more money until there's enough to go around again.

Have you ever wondered why it is that the world's richest continent – by far and away – is also the most backward and the poorest?

Africa has been metaphorically hanging out its collective begging bowl all my life; yet some of the world's greatest resources of diamond, platinum, gold, copper, natural gas, oil, coal, uranium and incredibly, fresh water, are there in abundance, along with a whole lot more.

So why is Africa so poor? Why are many of the children starving and the adults dying prematurely?

The answer is not what the western world governments want to hear, but that reply is also very much related to why the human race has not progressed positively as it should have done.

The short answer to why Africa is so poor is, governmental greed, corruption, and the artificial world market economy.

The long answer concerns the amoral greed of mining companies, improper payments to corrupt government officials on more than one continent; false, inflated debts levied against developing African nations, but perhaps above all, the general greed and corruption that exists within the western world's banking systems, other financial houses and all current associated private enterprise.

And that's only the short version of the long answer!

Most thinking people, who are not directly involved, have known for years just how unfair and corrupt the 'free market economics' of the world truly are.

One philosopher (James O'Dare 1946 – 2003) likened world economics to a mirror that the human race addictively stands before… "And observes its reflected, predatory, beast-like imperfections."

But the problem has always been; what can the democratic free market economy be replaced with?

Communism was the idealistic answer; sadly that turned out to be more corrupt and dictatorial than the class-infested, fault-filled regimes it replaced.

No matter what process is employed, someone has always got to be in charge.

Idealistically, we are all as good as each other and have a right to be here, principles I cherish, but we are not equal.

Many might not have been my physical equivalent when I was young; however, I suspect there are numerous individuals who are my intellectual superiors.

Some constantly have the acumen to profit while others see money slip through their open fingers like grains of fine sand.

A democratic system will always be preferable to any other method so far devised. Although the market forces and trade that accompany that process must change.

- A United World Government and the governments of member states should be free from financial encumberment.

- Planetary resources must be owned by everyone, irrespective of who owns the land they are on or under.

The rewards for ingenuity and entrepreneurialism need to remain, but in an altered form that does still ensure individual prosperity, both financially and socially; however, only to a point that is infinitely more realistic than exists today.

While fair compensation for landowners must exist, together with rewards for those that develop reserves, no members of society should profit excessively from resource exploitation.

When North Sea Oil was first discovered, the British Government of the day stated that once it was in full production, we would all enjoy greatly reduced, or even free, fuel in homes within the United Kingdom.

Echoes of Africa you may think?

Because it is a fact, only private companies profited from North Sea oil.

Of course, there are well crafted 'official reasons' and explanations – mostly to do with costs and privatisation – that glibly explain why fuel bills are still rising year by year... but I digress.

The important point to make is that rewards above a good living wage should only ever be given for innovation; even that remuneration should never supply someone with so much money they can have a marked effect on the world's economy or politicians.

The obscene blackmail perpetrated by, so-called, talented bankers, financial wizards and other 'giants of commerce', who threaten to leave their positions if they do not receive massive bonuses that amount to millions, should be criminalised.

Holding a world or country's economy to ransom should never be tolerated and must be challenged, the sooner the better.

- Private enterprise must have a place in a United World, or self-determination becomes farcical, but never to the point of having any influence upon democratic governance.

- Systems must be devised that allow unlimited funding for the future good and continuation of humanity.

~

There is one more very important point to be made about a United World and its administration.

A particularly well known saying declares 'power corrupts and total power corrupts totally'.

No government would ever have commanded so much power as a world administration with unlimited funding and total resource control.

The constitution, while a safeguard against dishonesty to a reasonable degree, could never be a complete panacea.

Therefore, the rewards for diligent government members must be above anything that has gone before – to a point where it would be impossible for corruption to be viable.

Yet still, no scheme that is devised by humans is perfect.

Despite the structure and systems I have sketched, sooner or later corruption will raise its repugnant head. Therefore, the punishments for such proven crimes must be as draconian as the rewards for diligent members are fantastic.

~

So there you have it!

A blueprint-philosophy for a future that would see a world population at least aware of the need for unity and unprecedented scientific progress.

The vision of a planet that could use its last valuable resources for the betterment and future of all humanity; not the continually multiplying personal wealth of a select few while the rest of the world slowly sinks into an abyss of pandemic and starvation.

What a breathtaking dream it is; a world with no major wars, no hunger and no divisive culture or religion; it leaves me with only one wonderful like-minded person's famous word...

Imagine! **(John Lennon 1940 – 1980)**

~

8

Epilogue

It may be that I have wasted my time. Perhaps I shall have been a fool.

Conceivably, this work will be ridiculed as simplistic or nonsensical. Feasibly, it will be viewed as more unrealistic than a journey to the stars themselves.

Or conversely, it will be declared no more than the ramblings of a bitter old man who no longer believes in anything and only wishes to insult everything.

If that is deemed to be the case, then I unreservedly apologise; because I have failed to get my message across.

There is no doubt in my mind that those who might ridicule or dismiss my ideas will number some intellectuals or perhaps even fanatics who run the world or influence those that do.

Ask yourself, if I am so wrong, why have more brilliant minds not come up with better plans for humanity's potential?

I've tried to show just how deeply humankind's faults and frailties run within us all – our superstitions and insecurities – how the unscrupulous use them as a controlling influence, when all we really need is the honest, common-sense, rule of law.

Then I examined how stupid all the manufactured differences between people truly are.

Of course we're all different, every one of us, it's just a matter of degree; and why should that make any difference?

Clearly, we cannot manage without each other.

No one will ever convince me that humanity does not need to strive for an alteration of direction.

Perhaps my idealistic philosophy for change is a goal set so far in the distance; it would be easy to describe it as a simplistic fantasy lacking the detail of realism.

Well, maybe it is, but look at the metaphoric signposts, they're all there at every turn of our lifetime journey; just try reading them.

I believe everything I've mentioned is factual and hopefully, unemotional; although I suspect, others might not agree.

But we are killing our planet, it's already terminally ill.

We do need to find more room, food and resources. Scientific advancement and space exploration are probably the only positive answers. So why not get on with it as a matter of priority – together?

I wish I could show you the faces of the future children; let you see their laughter and tears – sadly, I cannot.

Perhaps instead, look at your children, or your grandchildren – the joyful cacophony of a primary school playground.

Now imagine… think about how their offspring may smile. Will it be with the same coloured eyes that can look so appealingly innocent and trusting?

Will they maybe have the same shaped mouth that laughs so winningly?

If it were possible, could you perhaps see your 'long-ago' self still etched within their features?

Or will our future children not have enough to eat and room to live?

Conceivably, those children may curse the past generations – our generation… your generation – for seeing the signs of a world slowly but irrevocably being used up, destroyed and over-populated, yet doing almost nothing to stop it.

Maybe we might mouth the universal justification of, 'but what can I do about it? I'm only one person.'

A pathetic excuse, which will never be acceptable to those that follow.

Think! Use your brain, and then decide what you can do to save the world's future generations – and I don't mean popping empty milk cartons in the re-cycling sack either; although I suppose that's a start.

If you agree with any of my philosophy, then let it act as a springboard for your own ideas. Become involved with the community's political direction – or lack of it. Do not allow your Member of Parliament to enjoy his quiet privileged life.

Really, you know what needs doing, and if you don't, then read this book again.

~

Appendix 1

Summery of

<u>Prescriptive Philosophical Assertions.</u>

- Nobody can be cured of an addiction without first recognising and accepting that one exists.

~

- Human kind's greatest fault, frailty and obstacle against evolutional and social development is insecurity.

1. When contemplating any aspect of existence, the known universe, or infinity; there will always be an exception to any fact discovered, no matter how simple the fact, or how overwhelming the evidence may be supporting the fact. Nothing is ever accurately covered by one sweeping statement. No fact can ever be accepted without the reservation that all things are subject to incremental change, which by definition creates exception.

2. There is no totally conclusive evidence existing which suggests that anything is as it has always been, or always will be. No fact is ever entirely unambiguous. A truth today is often tomorrow's lie because acceptable evidence is a continually developing dynamic.

3. All facts depend upon the existence of a reality, which is an entirely subjective and altering entity. Reality, for human beings, cannot exist if someone is not there to observe it. Apparently, everyone's mind and awareness is different; therefore, reality is only ever a personal singularity.

~

- No ostensibly important fact can ever be believed by an intelligent person without viable evidence to support the fact. That burden of proof must be constantly re-examined in a systematic way that includes sound and dedicated practice to readjust pertinent fact so that it matches and supports the up-to-date reality.

- Any belief without evidence is an act of pure faith.

- I assert that anyone who accepts any serious fact to be true without evidence is perhaps, a fool and if asked, most people would say they would never do such a thing.

- Anyone who does not constantly re-examine any evidence that substantiates something of continuing vital importance – so big that it constantly affects our lives – is perhaps, an even bigger fool.

~

- Ask yourself a question. Why do all living things have an urge to perpetuate the species? It is my belief that there is no one definitive answer, other than natural instinct. We ignore such innate senses at our peril.

- Even life apparently incapable of reasoned thought has the natural instinct to propagate its species. The smaller the intelligence, the more singular are the instincts to survive and multiply.

- Leaving aside the additional in-depth and hypothetical question about an ability to reason, ask yourself, is our planet Earth alive? I believe that it is.

~

- The rule of law is probably the greatest virtue the human race possesses.

- Fish shoal, other animals herd for protection, and where the rule of law does not exist in a comprehensive and totally accepted way, humans tribe.

- The law must be nurtured, protected, unambiguous and never taken for granted; the more complexity the greater the insecurity.

- Insecurity is humankind's greatest frailty.

- The governing authorities and people of power and influence in all the countries throughout the world, either intentionally or unintentionally, aggressively or subliminally, constantly feed humanities' insecurities.

- The more we know about everything, the greater the fears and insecurities that accompany that awareness.

- The more we depend upon the unsubstantiated words of leaders and other influential individuals to feed our ingrained superstitions, the more insecure we become.

- The greater the insecurity, the bigger the emotional response.

- The workplace suffers from increased insecurity. Market forces, meeting targets and continually increasing profits have become Gods.

- Percentage wise, there are more people consulting psychiatrists and psychologists in the western world than there has ever been.

~

- Insecurity has caused abortive tribalistic, cultural and religious reliance that breeds divisiveness.

- Without otherwise altering feelings or emotions, were it possible to take away tribalism, cultural differences and religions, there would be no racism, only likes and dislikes.

- The divisiveness of culture, race and religion are the greatest manufacturers of insecurity.

~

- Where entrepreneurialism has influence or a significant effect over a large majority, such effect must be underpinned by a firm foundation of systematic practice that becomes more regulatory and influential than the originating entrepreneur.

- Global systemisation is the most logical and positive progression the human race could embrace.

~

- Every human is as good as each other and are born with a right to be here.

~

- There are always massive omissions with all the 'how everything started' theories and the accompanying equations.

- No sound, complete, evidential argument exists for how the universe began; where the constituents (God particle among other things) came from to start it, or how the space materialised to put it all in.

- I suggest there are two indisputable pieces of evidence that, at this time (2013) undoubtedly prove the reality of God to me.

- In the absence of any other evidential argument or rationalisation, the universe is God and is entirely inexplicable.

- Several philosophers' support the theory that the universe must have been created by God, just like a beautiful painting must have been created by an artist – nothing begets nothing, not something.

- God is a comfort. He's the old rag you chewed and held close as a child. He's the mystical being up in the sky who gives you a mental cuddle when you're scared witless. He must be contextualised as wholly incomprehensible and therefore only ever a very personal reality.

- Do not blame God for what you think he is or what you do with your portion of existence. If you can conceive God from the irrefutable substantiation I have illustrated, then you are responsible for your version of him.

- God is not a crutch to lean upon (we have minds of our own, so use them) but perhaps believing is a comfort when no other subsists.

- God is not an excuse to blame when things go wrong – we control enough of our lives and command enough factual evidence to know we humans or our unstable world and solar system are responsible.

- Look no further for an explanation of God, you will not find one.

~

- There is only one race and that is the human race.

- When you scrape away the basic similarities, stereotypical statements, and localised cultural desires for a tribal sameness – usually born of insecurities – every human being is unique and different.

- If there were no cultural differences, there would be no racism.

- There will always be prejudices – or to put it another way, likes and dislikes.

- The terms 'Black Man' and 'White Man' are political, discordant, based on culture diversity, negative historical record, physical inaccuracies and are utterly ridiculous.

- There are beautiful people of every shade of colour in terms of both looks and personality, just as there are ugly ones. It really is the same the whole world over. That is an evidential fact.

~

- The greater the threat to a community, country, or part of the world, the greater the unity between those threatened people.

- The natural instinct, bred from necessity, which caused homo-sapiens to first herd, then tribe, has bastardised into a destructive national parochialism that flourishes throughout the world. It must be changed.

- We are all uniquely different, but those singular physical and personality variations do not matter. We are one race – all the same – all human beings.

- If the world's population is to survive and flourish beyond the next century we must all strive for cultural sameness, not divisive difference – one race, one universal language.

- Communication, taken to the most sophisticated degree, where differences are hardly a noticed consideration – other than personal self-individuality – is the uniting force that can bring the world together.

- We must all share one vision and recognise that we do face an overwhelming threat greater than any peoples of the world has ever faced before.

- In order to meet that threat, universally shared objectives and ideals must become human ideology from the cradle to the grave.

~

- Individual likes and dislikes must always be nurtured and respected, but never to a degree where they can bring disharmony to a shared world culture.

- The world's population ought to be free to self-determine, but only as individuals. Where that self-determination has a harmful or extreme influence, it must be controlled and nullified.

- Culture is nothing more than a custom and practice that a majority decide to follow, usually started at the behest of one highly motivated, commanding and persuasive character.

- Another inexorable truth is that, due to the vast insecurities of human beings, nearly everyone feels they must belong to something.

~

- If a change is ever to be brought about, it must be fundamental and managed by the governments of the world's major countries, again not a unique event – if the threat is considered great enough.

- We are only limited by boundaries erected by the smallness of our minds.

- Flag waving nationalism is continually supported at every level of human existence and so are the antagonisms that accompany it.

- The mystic reverence subscribed to religions by almost every national government aids culturism and separatism.

- If humankind is to have a long-term potential, we must move towards one culture and the acceptance that we are all one race.

~

- If we do not manipulate change then it will surely manipulate us.

- There are only four kinds of change.

- Successful incremental alteration (resulting from a paradigm concept) on a worldwide scale should be expected to take decades, or even centuries.

~

- Sooner or later, all our lives depend on the skill of scientists.

- Humanity needs unity on a worldwide scale.

- Humanity needs more space to grow.

- Humanity needs a greater supply of resources without the crippling burden of artificial market-force expense.

- We need structured and fully resourced technological advancement that supports our growth and future resources; not the currently prioritised continuing research for yet another smart-phone, entertainment system or similar unimportant but nice-to-have high profit commodities.

~

- Expansionism on a planetary, then galactic scale is the only constructive conclusion for an ever increasing world population.

- Planetary and galactic colonisation can only succeed if the people of the Earth are united in that common cause.

- The world must be united – one official language that everyone understands.

- Only a united world with agreed long term objectives will guarantee the best possible chance for continued human existence.

~

- Very few people are capable of managing anything successfully over a protracted period without their authority and practice being underpinned by structure and system.

- Decade after decade of success never depends on an individual. It always depends upon the successful mandatory structure and systems put in place.

~

- The right to vote is one of the greatest freedoms enjoyed and supports the mass proposition of liberty and self-determination.

- Free speech and the right to vote for who governs us are the two founding necessities of any structure for world governance.

- A United World must have a clear mandatory structure and systems of practice to work within.

- A United World must be a democracy and have clear long-term objectives.

- All objectives must be mandatory statutes and be recorded in a constitution.

- The World Government must have all the powers currently bestowed upon any democratically elected national government that exists today (2013) but the originating constitution must only be subject to amendment.

- A constitution goes beyond the rule of law; it is the foundation from which fair and legitimate legislation springs.

- A constitution (with its accompanying amendments) becomes greater than the sum of a current government. It becomes the structure and guidance to govern by – the wisdom and experience of those that have gone before.

- Systems, by their very nature are authoritative habits.

- A constitution must clearly state all the major procedural rules for a world government.

- Elections ought to be held in constituent countries every five years.

- No elected World Government member should be permitted to serve more than two consecutive terms.

- World Government members should vote and elect a Head of State. That figurehead's only power above other members will be representational, holding a casting vote, and to call elections as constitutional time or circumstances dictate.

- Members ought to elect a Collator of Governance who will chair government sessions. The Chair will forgo the right to vote on all matters while in office, remaining non-executive and ideally, non-partisan.

- The Collator shall be responsible for order, discipline and verbatim records. The position will exist for a period no longer than the term of three governments.

~

- Social and cultural instruction within schools throughout the world ought to shape young minds to accept one official language, one race and the need for united expansionism on an interplanetary scale.

- All religious instruction should be limited to a similar position of subjects such as art and crafts. Nice to know topics, but of little importance for the majority of people in the real world and eventually, just a matter of personal choice and practice – no more than that.

- Education must, first and foremost, concentrate on filling the skill gaps created by world governmental policy and those of associated industries.

- All faith based schools ought to be closed and replaced by specialisations in the sciences so that the establishment of meaningful scientific research is created earlier and on a wider basis.

- The political definitions of black and white races should cease. Children must be taught that skin colour and facial features have no more significance than the colour of eyes or hair – a matter of personal taste along with personality likes and dislikes.

~

- I suggest funding and current fiscal expression is a false concept that, under its present connotation, should cease for the financing of a World Government and its business.

- The whole method of the current world economy is artificially created to produce a totally fictionalised fiscal reality. It is based on political practice, entrepreneurial cunning, greed, amoral tradition and dictatorial enforcement founded on tribalistic separatism.

- A United World Government and the governments of member states should be free from financial encumberment.

- Planetary resources must be owned by everyone, irrespective of who owns the land they are on or under.

- Private enterprise must have a place in a United World, or self-determination becomes farcical, but never to the point of having any influence upon democratic governance.

- Systems must be devised that allow unlimited funding for the future good and continuation of humanity.

~

www.ingramcontent.com/pod-product-compliance
Lightning Source LLC
Chambersburg PA
CBHW072139280526
45788CB00002B/698